The Mirror Within

A psychologist with several years' experience in educational counselling, Anne Dickson visited America in 1976 and trained in the field of sexual counselling. A major part of her work since then has been in this area, working with women and men in a wide variety of contexts. She is the author of *A Woman In Your Own Right: Assertiveness and You*, a best-selling book about the techniques of assertive behaviour. She considers assertiveness and sexuality as especially pertinent to the changing role of women in our society. She has set up an association to train other women to teach these skills throughout the UK and Ireland.

Anne Dickson's other works include the acclaimed *Menopause: The Woman's View*, co-written with classical homoeopath Nikki Henriques.

Also by Anne Dickson and published by Quartet Books

A WOMAN IN YOUR OWN RIGHT: *Assertiveness and You*

MENOPAUSE: *The Woman's View* (with Nikki Henriques)

The Mirror Within

A New Look at Sexuality

Anne Dickson

Illustrated by Kate Charlesworth

Quartet Books

First published by Quartet Books Limited 1985
A member of the Namara Group
27/29 Goodge Street, London W1P 1FD

Copyright © 1985 by Anne Dickson
Reprinted 1987, 1988 (twice), 1989, 1990, 1991, 1992, 1995

British Library Cataloguing in Publication Data
Dickson, Anne
 The mirror within: a new look at sexuality.
 1. Woman—Sexual behaviour
 I. Title
 612'.6'0088042   HO29

 ISBN 0-7043-3474-7

Phototypeset by AKM Associates (US) Ltd.
Ajmal House, Haynes Road, Southall London
Printed and bound in Great Britain by
BPC Paperbacks Ltd
A member of
The British Printing Company Ltd

For Nikki,
whose love has seen me through

Contents

Contents

Acknowledgements

I would like to acknowledge my appreciation of the following people: Deidre Sanders who encouraged me to write the original synopsis and who has given me a lot of practical and emotional support; Shirley Conran, Blaize Davies, Felicity Green, Lyn Lewis, Grania Luttman-Johnson and Carolyn Smith who shared their ideas with me in discussions on various aspects of the book; Elizabeth Adeline, Kay Barwick, Tricia Cameron, Candida Capone, Breda Hill, Pat Hislop, Judith Jenner, Jane Macdonald, Nuria Pompeia, Gill Simon and Kath Swift who are among those who have contributed to the content; Tirth Flora, Antonia Hammond, Janet Hibbert, Jeanette Hitchcock, Rabia Nadeem, Kanta Patel, Patt Purdy, Nickie Roberts, Susie Sanders, Jeannie Sperry and Linzi Weames who agreed to be interviewed and who helped to give substance to my thoughts when my confidence failed me.

I would also like to thank those people who very kindly took the time to read and make valuable and critical comments on different parts of the manuscript: Liz Clasen, Patricia Gillan, Nikki Henriques, Breda Hill, Jane Macdonald, Clare Manifold, Jonathan Pincus, Peter Reason, Rick Sanders and Wendy White; to Janet Law, my editor, whose gentle and persistent encouragement kept me going when my resolution wavered; to Stella Salem for ploughing through pages of illegible text with good humour and for her important and helpful insights; to those women in RWTA who have sent me many messages of love and support in written and psychic form; to the cat, the tree and the lizard who continue to sustain me in their different ways; to all those women, past and present, whose words have inspired, confronted, comforted and encouraged me.

Finally, I would like to acknowledge my grandmothers, Dorothy Dickson and Yvonne Earle, who both died before I could get to know them but nevertheless for whom I feel a very special link and love.

The Mirror Within

1

Introduction

This book is a challenge. It won't tell you how to find a partner. Nor is it a sex manual. It will, however, question some basic assumptions about human sexuality and about women's sexuality in particular.

For many of us, sexuality represents a very private part of our lives. Overexposure in the media lulls us into a superficial sense of ease with the subject, but when it comes to personal experience and personal feelings, the lid comes firmly down. This is why it is so difficult for attitudes to change. Rarely do we go deep enough to excavate the foundations of our beliefs, and we merely tamper with the super-structure. The experiences recounted in this book come, for the most part, from various groups and classes I have worked with over the past eight years.

My initial attraction to working in this area springs from personal experience. Twenty years ago, as a young adult, I had been given no information about sex at all either at home or at school. I was totally reliant on school friends' discussions and fumblings in the dark. Ignorance did mean innocence for a short while, but it was soon converted to inadequacy when my first lover indicated that there was something wrong because I didn't have an orgasm. Things went downhill from there as I became more inadequate and more confused, still waiting for a man to make it all happen. Then, ten years ago, I learned the relevance of the clitoris to a woman's experience of orgasm. I find it difficult to believe now but, prior to that, I had no idea at all of the existence of my clitoris. That moment of discovery was quite memorable. Something shifted very deep inside and for a while inadequacy was converted into rage. Why the hell hadn't I been told before? I felt full of blame and resentment towards past male lovers who had criticized but not helped. It didn't dawn on me that I could have found out for myself. This discovery and the achievement of the Big O injected me with a renewed sexual vigour plus independence – but the attraction soon palled. I felt like somebody who, after straining to compete in a particular race and finally being allowed to enter, realizes halfway along that she doesn't want to be running in that race at all. My personal and professional confusion continued until the second major breakthrough which occurred in one particular sexuality workshop. Halfway through the morning, a woman who had introduced herself as a sister in a religious community suddenly burst into tears. She said she felt very alone because the other women were referring to their relationships and she didn't have one. However, she still felt sexual and found it very frustrating not to be able to express this because it did not fit in with conventional ideas. As we talked, I asked her if she could find a way to affirm her own sexuality; how did she celebrate and express her sexual self? She smiled and said, 'I pray naked.' Her reply embodied a truth whose simplicity struck in me a chord of delight and humility which I will never forget. Her statement suddenly made clear what I had been struggling with for some time: that, all too often, we find ourselves stuck with rigid norms and fixed ideas about what sexuality means. Also, we can become so immersed in doing things 'right' that we lose sight of the fact that sexuality is an important aspect of *self* expression. It follows then that like everything else which concerns our self-image, it is easy to feel we have to conform!

Our sexual feelings take us into an intimate and private realm of being, which, in principle, should be intact and free from external demands. Yet, this most intimate, central aspect of ourselves is subject to the same erosion as are the more peripheral areas of our lives; erosion by demands, either real or imagined, to be someone other than we are. In this deepest and most vulnerable part of ourselves, we have learned to conform and to compete, to compare and to achieve, to pretend and to adapt. The lack of self-esteem which most women share is significantly affected by the fact that we do not have even this part of ourselves, to ourselves. Many of us lose touch with our spontaneity and make do with an image we have modelled out of the different parts we have learned will reward us with acceptance and love. This is where the lessons of assertiveness are so relevant to women's sexuality.

Every day, many women are taking steps, large and small, towards regaining more control over their lives. In our homes we're beginning to see that the chores can be shared – they are not our intrinsic duty. We are beginning to set limits. At work, we're not so acquiescent when being walked over or ignored. We are beginning to realize our worth. We're beginning to reclaim the validity of our intuition – if something *feels* wrong, then we know it's likely to *be* wrong, despite rational arguments to the contrary. We're trusting our feelings and are more able to acknowledge them truthfully whatever they may be; consequently we feel stronger, not weaker as we had feared. We are learning that a clear, direct, unwavering approach is much more effective in the long run than a vicious swipe. We are making the important discovery that we do not have to resort to the masculine stereotype of aggression and insensitivity as the only alternative to wimpish ways! We can care deeply for someone and still bravely speak the truth. In many areas of our lives, we have stopped waiting for permission. In short, we are becoming more spontaneous. We are becoming more ourselves as we respond, reach out, participate or withdraw.

This confidence and a growing sense of self spreads into every area of our lives, into all the situations in which we interact with other human beings. But one area remains exceptionally difficult: our sexuality and our sexual relationships.

Many of us find asserting ourselves in sexual relationships very tricky. First, we are extremely vulnerable. Most times a sexual partner is someone we are very close to and our involvement with that person is a complex one. The sexual threads interweave with other aspects of our lives together. Feelings run deep and we're not going to want to jeopardize our relationship or risk doing anything which might mean that we will lose that person's love. Holding on to the security of a relationship and the certainty that we are loved by another feels safer than taking the risk of speaking our minds or expressing our true feelings. It's easier to push the disappointment, the fear, the frustration to a remote part of our minds and to be thankful for what we have.

A second difficulty is confusion. One of the golden rules of assertive communication is to be clear about what we want before asking for it. Many of us are more confused about our feelings, our responses, our needs and our desires in a sexual context than in any other part of our lives. How can we assert our needs sexually when we find it impossible to explain or justify them? We feel odd or freakish, and if we do take the initiative and ask a partner for more affection and touching, how can we persist when we are met with incom-

3

prehension or a blank refusal? Many women find it impossible to express their convictions in words, so they often let the subject drop and find another outlet for those needs, or even deny them altogether.

Saying no is more difficult when we feel responsible for someone else's arousal or feel helpless because we can't explain our lack of interest in sex even to ourselves at that moment, never mind to a bewildered or irritated partner. Or, when a man of recent acquaintance starts making moves which are overtly sexual, a woman may feel confused – she thought she was just being friendly and although the boundaries may have been quite clear to her, it's obvious they weren't to him. But how difficult it is to be decisive and persistent when, in our hearts, we're really unsure which signals we have or haven't been giving.

Handling any situation assertively means moving from a base of self-esteem, anchored deeply within ourselves. Only then can we risk the disruption and awkwardness, the disapproval or reproach which sometimes result from new and unfamiliar behaviour. Far from being rooted in self-esteem, we tend to flounder on a ground of self-doubt and uncertainty, and most of all we tend to silence. This makes it difficult to talk even to a close friend. We assume that people 'do it' successfully but don't talk about it explicitly. Many women hesitate to discuss their relationships because they feel they are betraying their sexual partners. So we don't share honestly and we don't learn. There is nothing we can read, no one we can talk to, no one who can love us enough to allow us to avoid working it out individually for ourselves.

The challenge is enormous: trying to extricate ourselves from the sexual norms, pressures and mayhem of the culture around us and restoring a sense of our own powerful and integrated sexuality takes a long time. For most women the resistance is enormous as well! It's much easier to find 101 more important things to do with your life than look at your sexuality. Easier to believe that things are better left buried. It feels like a minefield, which it is at times. But, to start, it means that you must think enough of yourself to take a look into the unfamiliar. It feels like a big step – which it is – but living in this time of transition, I know of no more radical step to take.

2
Landscape

When I was asked what this book was about I replied, 'Women's sexuality.' 'Oh yes,' or 'I see', were the usual responses, although it was clear that nobody really knew what I meant.

The two words do seem inadequate to convey the scope of a subject which touches so many other areas of our lives. What it means to us individually will inevitably reflect our own particular experience. Imagine a group of women of different ages and expectations discussing what women's sexuality means to them:

It's about the fulfilment of having children.
You have to take a man in hand and teach him to be a good lover.
I have twenty orgasms every time!
An instrument of male oppression.
You have to be pretty and fall in love and get married and have a
    sex life and a wonderful family.
Women are much better lovers than men.
What *is* the difference between a clitoral and vaginal orgasm
    anyway?
I don't know anything about it: you had better ask my husband.
I was interfered with as a child and never got over it.
It's very powerful, we beat the men hands down!
It's too late for me now – I wish I'd had your freedom today.
If you remove the phallic symbol, then the sex is magic!
My boyfriend got me pregnant, I had an abortion and now I am
    frigid.

5

It's all very overrated and over-discussed. There are much more important things to life than *that*.

All of this is true and more. Although it is an area of strong personal beliefs and values, we often find that our experience is shared. In order to understand this experience, we need to know a little of the circumstances in the past which affect our present.

A mixture of religious, social and political trends over the past 2,000 years have provided us with a cultural backcloth against which each of us attempts to make sense of our own lives. A brief glimpse of images of female sexuality in the past can help us understand more about the personal challenges we face today. And, more important, it can help to show how we might begin to make changes for the future.

The most deeply ingrained attitudes include those encouraged by the teachings of Christianity and Judaism. Their hallmark can still be found at the root of thinking about female sexuality today – the twin faces of evil and chastity.

The moral of the story is clear: Eve's behaviour in the Garden of Eden left no one in any doubt as to woman's potential. She seduced an innocent man by consorting with the devil and thus brought eternal damnation to all humanity. On one hand, sex was envisaged as the devil's dynamite, a constant power in a man's genitals, ready to be kindled in an instant by the tempting wiles of a woman. Or, on the other hand, the devil (and sexuality) was believed to reside in a woman's flesh; women's bodies were vehicles of evil, carriers of an evil force. Either way, women had to be avoided at all cost. The burning of a million women as witches in Europe throughout the fifteenth, sixteenth and seventeenth centuries bears grim testimony to the fear and hatred of women and their attributed powers.

But this image of evil had a second face. These very same bodies were also vehicles for future offspring, then much needed for enlarging families and extending power. One of the fascinating things about human beings is that when a deeply held conviction is challenged by a piece of information that doesn't fit, this challenge creates a stress which can be alleviated only by reconstructing another image that incorporates *both* elements at once. Letting go the conviction is too frightening, so we develop a way to let both pieces of information reside comfortably together in our minds. These opposing beliefs – woman's body as potentially evil *and* as a necessary social vehicle – had to be reconciled. Consequently, an alternative model emerged which represented the opposite of evil; an image which was pure, innocent and could conceive in such a way as to bypass the necessity for contact with the flesh. Thus, the two faces of the virgin/whore, of Mary/Eve, took root in the human imagination.

Chastity was a necessity in a society in which an individual's future was based on family expansion and inherited wealth. It was considered crucial to ensure pure-bred sons who would carry on the line, and the unsullied nature of the line meant that the woman who bore those children had to be unsullied herself. Chastity became the supreme virtue.

Moreover, the function of motherhood had to be built into the institution of the family in such a way as to provide a focal point for a woman's energies – her physical and emotional and sexual energies could be properly harnessed and controlled if they were devoted to that end. Within the family, potential evil could be transformed into good. Later on, this goodness even became holy. During the rise of evangelical religion throughout Europe 200 years ago, women became highly involved in church activities. They filled the pews and became the standard bearers of the moral vanguard. A new female stereotype emerged – of a nature which expressed itself through moral superiority, virtue, patience and long-suffering devotion to others. This refinement still exists today in attempts to shield women from sights too violent, words too obscene, affairs too worldly and positions too responsible!

With the growth of scientific investigation, the medical profession assumed the authority which had previously belonged to the church. All parts of the body were dissected, analysed and labelled, and a woman's reproductive system was no exception. As the womb was found to be at the *physical* centre of a woman's body, it seemed clear to the scientists that this provided a physical explanation for woman's maternal nature: the womb was the focal point of her body and her reproductive function was the emotional focus of her life. Her womb physically and emotionally governed her life. These findings reinforced popular attitudes and opinions.

As the respiratory, digestive and circulatory systems were investigated, so too was the system of sexual response, which yielded its own category of abnormalities, diseases and pathologies. Physiological experiments confirmed the psychological discoveries of Freud: sex basically belonged to men but, at the same time, women were believed to be governed by a physical and sexual impulse to bear children. Any form of sexual expression outside conception was regarded as abnormal, immature, hysterical or insane. Masturbation was one example of 'abnormal expression'.

As discussions of Freudian ideas fanned belief that sex was a monstrous urge which a man struggled unsuccessfully to control from birth to death, it was reassuring that his dutiful wife, the mother of his children, could save him; she could tame these wild excesses and, what is more, transform a basically ugly bodily need into something sacred by conceiving and bearing his children – a service of spiritual salvation. She was placed on an even higher pedestal at the centre of the family and the centre of the home. Her role was crucial to the maintenance of society.

What happened to the other face? The 'evil' one? She didn't disappear. On the contrary, it is known that at the time when the mother/holy wife image was at the peak of its popularity, there were more thousands of prostitutes than ever before. Men would visit them to avoid 'troubling' their wives. And these women were not valued, but were considered as a necessary curse – a troubling reminder of men's baser nature – and despised as a consequence. This contempt was exhibited by the casual police attitude towards Jack the Ripper's victims. Somehow, even today, it is not as bad to kill a 'prostitute' as it is to kill a 'student' or 'churchgoer' or 'mother of three'.

In post-Victorian times, sex provided a popular talking point, as it does today. Children, previously thought to be innocent, were seen as being sexual; sex became synonymous with sexual activity (fantasy, desire, genital contact, arousal, ejaculation). The early sex researchers contributed a lot to a more frank and open discussion of what people did together. Women were now seen as capable of sexual arousal. Female sexuality was defined in the context of marital intercourse, in keeping with the wifely role, but nevertheless a woman was permitted to have some pleasure of her own. This was a significant change from a 'sexless' nature: now wives were encouraged to be sexual, responsive companions to their husbands.

In the past thirty years, there has been a mushrooming of statistical, wide-scale research into the topic of human and animal sexual behaviour. Sex research has provided irrefutable evidence that women can enjoy a sexual life apart from bearing children. In fact, far from having a capacity inferior to a man's, a woman's sexual capacity was pronounced superior – she could enjoy more orgasms, had more staying power than a man and her sexual behaviour was less affected by the process of aging.

Social trends have also changed. In secular western societies, chastity has become less important during the last fifty years, although virginity is still a prerequisite for marriage in many countries governed by the Catholic, Muslim or Hindu religions. Chastity was important when the blood-line was crucial but, since most of us do not depend on inherited money or property, it has become more acceptable to have sexual partners before marriage. But the much-publicized concern in Britain before the heir to the throne was married in 1981, shows that chastity will always be an issue when sufficient wealth and status depend on it.

Research proved that women's bodies were no handicap in terms of their sexual ability, and with the contraceptive pill, even less so. For most unmarried women, there was less need for restraint. This information confronted the traditional beliefs about women – here was a woman who enjoyed sex, but outside the context of marriage and motherhood. How then could the potential power of her body be constrained?

A solution emerged with a change of emphasis from the virgin to the whore, but with a modern face. I call her Superlay. She embodied all the new 'facts' about women. She could have sex without getting pregnant because of the pill. She could have sex with both men and women, anything, in fact. Superlay was always available and willing. She knew exactly how to please her man: she was randy, could come at the drop of a trouser, take the initiative, plead for it, beg for it and play his game to a tee. A very exciting partner in fact, just what every man wanted – all the fun without the responsibility!

Superlay offered an altogether more sexually *active* image, but it was no more liberated. Her unbridled sexual appetite didn't free her from dependence. Born of male fantasy, her very reason for being was her ability to please her man. Her body had no intrinsic beauty and her glory, alas, was still reflected. So this most recent image still does not represent a woman who is sexual in her *own* right.

After-effects

The two most powerful threads which link the past to the present are, first, that a woman's body is central to her personality and behaviour and, second, that a woman's body is intrinsically *bad*. According to this viewpoint, the physical characteristics of a woman's body offer a clear indication of what are expected to be her sexual, social and emotional characteristics. There are all sorts of obvious examples: if her body can endure the pain of childbirth, she will be able to endure all sorts of other hardships. A maternal function indicates a maternal nature. If her body needs to be restrained and subdued, her social power and influence will need to be restrained and subdued.

Since women are very much affected by their bodily rhythms and processes, the connection is a true one – but unfortunately the connection is contaminated by negativity and guilt. It is difficult for a woman to avoid the disabling effects of this legacy. It often distorts her own view of her body, and her attitudes to her intellect, her feelings, her spirit and her sexuality. Although this distortion will be affected by a woman's particular culture, it is significant that women from many very differing cultures and countries have one thing in common: millions of women feel badly about their bodies. Deep, deep within, a multi-lingual voice convinces women that they should not like or value their bodies and that a woman's body is not a blessing but a curse.

When women in a western society talk of their relationship with their bodies, several shared themes emerge.

Apology. 'If only I could just find the *perfect* pair of jeans.' Subjected to a constant barrage of media images of youth and beauty, women often feel that their bodies lack intrinsic beauty or value and a lot of effort goes into the correction of natural deficits. This low self-image spreads to all areas of women's lives.

Tension. 'I want to show I'm interested but not *too* interested.' Have you ever felt you have to get it just right, that you have to measure up to some internal ideal? It can feel like being in a tug of war, trying to stand upright between the opposing requirements of chastity and lust, between self-sacrifice and self-indulgence, between being maternal and sexual, between being receptive and active, between self and others. The ever-present watchfulness that is needed to prevent us from being pulled too far to one side or the other produces a state of constant tension. This tension causes a physical and a psychological stress which makes it very difficult to be spontaneous. We become inhibited in our voices, our movement, our gestures and our sexual response; we become inhibited from expressing our thoughts, feelings and opinions.

Dependence. 'Bend me, shape me, anyway you want me, as long as you love me, it's all right.' Have you ever felt grateful to someone for selecting you to love and to hold? Sometimes we can find ourselves being so dependent on someone else's approval and permission that any action which puts that approval in jeopardy can seem too risky. We often wait for a partner to bring us to life with a touch, to rescue us and make us beautiful. We can also depend on someone else for mental and emotional stimulation, for rescue from being a nonentity: being loved by another becomes a sign of social status and significance.

Alienation. 'I never seem to know what I'm feeling until it's too late.' Many women cut themselves off from their bodies. With little inner motivation to enjoy or understand them, it is easy to undervalue and underrate the natural rhythms and moods and processes of a woman's body. With labels such as 'hysteria' or 'incapacity' or 'sickness' it is not a surprise that many women have become very defensive about this part of their being. The tragedy is that we have lost touch with a central part of our strengths as women – we have lost touch with our moods, our resources, our responses, our dreams, our intuition, our emotions. We have learned to devalue this part of ourselves as well, so we listen less and less to the inner wisdom of our bodies.

Invisibility. Many women find it difficult to embrace their sexuality wholeheartedly when sex is associated with so much that is offensive and inhuman and plainly ridiculous. If it isn't violent, it can all be so earnest! Where is the happy medium between the romantic nonsense of Prince Charming and the creation of lifesize inflatable dolls as vehicles of sexual release!

Antidotes

Sex has become institutionalized in our culture and like our other institutions it bears little imprint of a female perspective. Sex has also become a commodity characterized by conquest, genitality and goals. Many women wish the focus wasn't always on the genitals, that intercourse didn't always have to be the begin and end all, that sex doesn't have to be set apart from everything else in life.

A woman's perspective on the subject of sexuality is fairly difficult to envisage and difficult to talk about precisely because it has become so invisible. Starting off a process of enquiry into this complex subject means recognizing these themes at work to a greater or lesser extent in our lives. It can be helpful to keep in mind some positive alternatives.

Pride. Starting from the centre and working outwards, we can develop a positive approach towards our bodies and begin to take pride in our individual beauty instead of bowing to the pressures of unfavourable comparison.

Choice. Knowing our bodies well can lead to a much deeper self-acceptance. Instead of worrying about which ideal we should be aiming for, we can look carefully at what we have learned and what we want to discard. We can move from a position of choice rather compulsion.

Responsibility. The realization that our sexuality is not something which can be given or taken away from us by another person, that it is something unique, can help us to take responsibility for our own needs and expression, instead of waiting for rescue and redemption. Being responsible and more confident in this particular area of our lives has a ripple effect.

Integration. This is a crucial part of building a positive self- and body-image. We can heal the split between body and mind, between body and genitals, between sexuality and the rest of our lives.

Open celebration. With encouragement and permission we can celebrate a part of ourselves which has become so negated. Sharing with other women honestly and openly reduces our feelings of isolation. Sharing can also help us to support rather than compete with each other. Openly celebrating our own form of sexual expression need not be blatant – it has much more to do with what is *inside* – it need not be constructed around outside norms and expectations.

Before leaving this historical review, I must add that it is encouraging to read of research which suggests that this story did not start with the effect of Christianity. There is growing evidence from thousands of years before which indicates a culture based on a system of inheritance in which women, not men, were the principle figures. My imagination has been fired by the evidence of a way of life so totally different from our own: women were considered first-class citizens; women were honoured, cherished and valued because their bodies were honoured, cherished and valued; their shapes were woman-shaped and natural. Women held no doubt about their beauty, within and without, and sexuality was expressed by women and men in a way that celebrated life. I like to think that there is at least one gene in me which is a throwback to those times – the thought inspires me when I most despair and reminds me that there has to be another way to live.

3
Close-up

One of the first things to do in an exploration of our sexuality is to understand how we have learned to behave in the way we do. We are not always conscious of ideals although most of us are often uncomfortably aware that we fall short in some way. As we grow up we will have learned that being a woman and being sexual has many meanings – some positive and encouraged, others negative and criticized or punished. We hear different direct and indirect messages from our parents, our peers, the media, and in our minds we construct an ideal code of conduct which is modified with later experience.

The difference between sexual learning and every other kind of learning is that the subject is taboo – we learn very little fact and an awful lot of fiction! And, as adults, we are not encouraged to discuss this subject openly. This means that we are left with a confusion of messages and expectations which are very difficult to sort out on our own. It is only when we can talk about these things that we begin to discover what is still relevant to our lives and what has become redundant.

Faulty learning can be clarified by information. If we put information next to myth, then we can decide what we are going to believe. If we are not clear which is which, we will continue to be propelled by 'shoulds' and 'oughts' rather than by choice.

Images

Some of the messages we carry around in our heads are unique to our own experience. But from listening to many women's descriptions of their conflicts and beliefs about their sexuality, it is possible to identify several models in our culture. These are presented here not as examples of real human beings but as caricatures, as female sexual stereotypes. First, there are the stereotypes which offer different aspects of women as basically non-sexual beings.

Virgin. The virginal image portrays a woman's body as property or territory – at a premium when untouched, devalued after someone has set foot there and made his mark. And the transition hinges on one action alone: penetration. When physically intact and whole, the Virgin is a child – her body is pure, her naïve head empty of knowledge. She is encouraged not to know too much about sex, never to talk about it.

Romantic Heroine. This heroine is beautiful, certainly, but the 'most ravishing' will be the 'most ravished', so beware! She will pay for her beauty by having to suffer. She accepts this as her fate and the one thing that will keep her going through all manner of peril and adversity will be the light of hope that one day she will be rescued. In the nick of time, Mr Right is there – he has money, status, a title, power to shelter her from the storm, to protect her from further harm. She is safe at last, rewarded with the happy ending she so clearly deserves for 'putting up with so much' in her life.

Madonna. The Madonna gazes at her infant, adoring and adored, their shared intimacy superseding and often excluding any other. She is at her emotional and physical peak: her body is redeemed from sin. She achieves sexual and personal fulfilment through motherhood alone. Sex therefore holds no intrinsic interest or pleasure for her but is a means of reproduction. She offers sanctuary between her thighs or in her arms, or at her breast – her sexual pleasure is not direct but she achieves the indirect satisfaction of nurturing another and knowing she is a harbour for her man. This is her pleasure.

Think of England. This derives from the familiar phrase 'Just lie back and think of England' which apparently encouraged a woman to fulfil her conjugal duty and offer it up for the Empire. This woman accepts there is no physical pleasure for her but she can lie there and know she is fulfilling her duty! She acquiesces to her partner's needs out of love, compassion or duty because she knows it is expected as part of a wife's sexual role.

Then there are the stereotypes which depict woman as basically sexual.

Whore. As the mythical opposite of the Virgin, the Whore has made the transition from purity of thought, word and deed to sexual knowledge and experience. Her body is now sullied and spoiled. As Virgin she represented a prize, as Whore she is no longer of value because her body, her territory has been possessed by another. Being no longer a real catch, her body has a 'hand-me-down' quality. She promises access: she is 'fair game'.

Prostitute. For all her technique and availability, the Prostitute still shows no signs of sexual pleasure. She, too, can be understanding, even maternal, in her acceptance of men's bizarre needs. The difference is that she charges money. She knows that sexual favours have a price and therefore a man in need gives her bargaining power.

Nymphomaniac. This is the woman whose sexual needs can never be satisfied. She is obsessed and insatiable and no amount of penile thrusting will ever fill her up. This desire is unhealthy because it is uncontrolled and has taken her over. When insatiability is not associated with the devil it is seen as mental illness, which is why we find her in clinical case studies of 'abnormal' sexual behaviour.

Eve. Now part of Christian tradition, Eve represents the siren, the mermaid on the rocks whose voice lures men to their doom. No man can resist her. Women like her, with their beauty, charm and seductive wiles, are responsible for the fall of countless noble and virtuous men throughout history. Instead of taming the sexual monster as the Madonna does, she invites and encourages it to emerge, enticing it to its doom!

17

Slave. Her hands are bound, she kneels, her face to the floor. The stirring in her loins reminds her that she is a slut: she is not the refined, aloof princess she once thought she was. She begs her master to take her. He tells her to wait. She pleads with him. He curses her and makes her wait. She writhes in agony and begs him again. He holds her brutishly and enters her. She should feel degraded and shamed but she is moved and excited. She screams in submission and pleasure. She cannot hold back any more, she begs to yield and gives herself to him. This is her master, to whom she belongs. She hopes he will care a little for his slave. He has told her that inside every woman, if one can find it, is a natural slave. She believes him!

Superlay. This more modern stereotype dates from the 1960s. We find her in books and magazine articles entitled 'How to be a perfect lover' or 'How to please your man and prevent him from straying'. And certainly she is the one to know. She is ready for anything, any time – she will readily accommodate her partner, knowing exactly how to turn him on. Her partners are usually men although, being 'laid back', she is used to going with women as well, as long as it doesn't involve emotional closeness. She comes easily and often – she is lusty but cool. Her performance is, in a word, perfect.

Black Widow. This stereotype is named after a spider because of the mating ritual of this particular insect: the female attracts her mate, is fertilized by him and after penetration, injects him with a fatal poison. This woman is basically a castrator. She castrates by sexual and social domination, destroying a man's power. She feels a sense of triumph once she has 'got' a man: she will arouse him, get him to penetrate and ejaculate inside her as a way of establishing her power over him.

These stereotypes constructed around the Virgin/Whore model are heterosexual in their assumptions. Less obvious in their influence, but equally powerful, are the lesbian stereotypes. The lesbian is a woman who has all the sexual connotations of being a woman but, in addition, makes love with other women. This clashes with the assumption that a woman's sexuality depends on the presence of a man. The apparent contradiction has led to the cultural construction of lesbian stereotypes, some of which are described here. Again, it is important to remember that they are caricatures which do not exist but which influence our imagination and hence our perceptions of ourselves as women.

Marauding Dyke. She is more like a man than a woman. You used to be able to spot her a mile off, an older woman, stomping around, short-haired, deep-voiced, wearing a suit or overalls and heavy boots. Now she may be more sophisticated, probably a ruthless and successful career woman, but she's still up to the same tricks. She behaves sexually like a man and prowls around the bars and discos on the look-out for her prey: some inexperienced, younger victim whom she is out to seduce.

Tragic Misfit. This lesbian is a child who has never grown up to be a woman. She is immature, stuck in the adolescent phase. She is emotionally unstable and so tormented by her difference that her future is inevitably doomed. She has become one of society's unfortunates. Whether the cause is a genetic imbalance or a distorted experience in childhood or that she just cannot pull a man, there is always something *wrong*.

Superdyke. This lesbian is a man-hater. 'Do you know they're already planning all-female cities?' men whisper in horror! Superdyke is the ideal lesbian feminist and ideologically correct. She completely rejects heterosexual norms, values, symbols, behaviour and men.

You may be wondering 'What on earth has any of this to do with *me*?' Remember, they are extremes and so, although you won't see yourself exactly, you may be interested to discover some of the messages about women's sexuality which derive from these stereotypes. As with any other area of our lives, we model our behaviour on outside examples. This is why, like it or not, we find that these sexual images affect our attitudes towards our bodies, our sexual response and our sexual relationships. As you read through the next section, see if you can identify some of the messages from these models which may have affected your own assumptions without your knowing.

Reflections

Virgin. Our definition of a virgin today is a woman whose vagina has not been penetrated by a penis in intercourse. By extension, this defines sexual as sexually active and sexually active as having intercourse. We have a clear blueprint for the popular conviction that a woman isn't a woman without a man – she has no sexuality of her own.

Where does this leave women who are adult virgins today? They often find it difficult to affirm virginity as a positive option in the face of a culture which suggests that a virgin is a woman who just 'hasn't made it'. Older women and women who are religious celibates are also dismissed as non-sexual, not having a sexuality of their own, simply because it is obvious that they don't have a sexual relationship.

Women can also feel caught between the two poles of virgin and whore. We may not want to appear too easy or too ready to acquiesce to sexual demands. On the other hand, we don't want to look too unwilling or too distant, as a complete brush-off risks giving the wrong impression. We find difficulty in saying a clear no when we are reluctant to appear *too* pure and *too* unavailable.

Romantic Heroine. The success
of romantic fiction today proves
without a doubt that the
Romantic Heroine has an
enormous appeal for millions of
women. The message is powerful
and clear: underneath we are all
the same, ripe for seduction by
the right man. Even the
intelligent heroines succumb
eventually! Because of this we
will have to suffer in some way.
This image offers a clear
enticement to masochism:

suffering will pay off because, in the end, Mr Right will fix it.

We all escape into daydreams at times for fun, but how deeply do we hang on to the hope of rescue? How many of us are sometimes reluctant to take responsibility and face up to the reality of a situation because we are waiting for someone else to do it for us? We are further encouraged to depend on men, not only for rescue from the fate of being unwed but from all kinds of different situations. However strong we are, we can still feel the pull to revert to what we believe to be our basic helplessness.

Suffering becomes dangerously glamorous. Many of us persist in adverse circumstances simply because of the addiction to that glamour – we believe that if we can just keep going, our struggles will one day be noticed and rewarded. And we can also find it difficult to extricate ourselves from emotionally crippling or sterile relationships because we would have to face up to feeling cheated of the happy ending we were promised. And after a break-up, we often feel an emotional and social failure because we did not manage to live 'happily ever after'.

Madonna. The Madonna image
encourages the excessively
maternal, and over-nurturing
behaviour which can adversely
affect sexual activity. Women
who describe men as 'little boys'
often treat them as such in bed
and out. The Madonna suggests

to a wife that her husband is another of her children – that he needs to be protected from his feelings and from her feelings and always has to be comforted when needy. The problem is that if a woman does want to assert her own needs, how can she do so when she sees her primary role as that of providing an emotional and sexual outlet for the man instead of seeing herself in a sexual relationship with an *equal* partner?

Think of England. While none of us may have consciously offered up any sexual encounter for King and Country, this image still affects our current experience. Women can enjoy a partner getting pleasure from their bodies but actually experience no direct enjoyment themselves. We sometimes feel absent from our bodies, or accept that our bodies are a vehicle for another person's pleasure. We feel that our partners have a right to intercourse within a married or committed relationship, even if we don't feel like it ourselves.

If you've ever found it difficult to say no to a sexual partner because it conflicted with what you felt were their rights or found yourself 'putting up with' sex, you'll recognize the power of this message.

Whore. The 'spoiled' image of the Whore can mean that if a woman has been known to have had sexual experience, it is assumed that she is naturally more available. Women who have been married at one time but are now divorced or widowed can find themselves confronted with exactly this assumption: since there is no man around, she must be missing 'it' and since one penis is as good as another, she can find herself on the receiving end of several unwanted offers of service!

The root of the prejudice that a married woman faces if she tries to convince anyone that she has been raped by her husband is identical to that faced by many prostitutes if they try to complain to the police that they have been raped or attacked by their clients. The implication is that, unless 'virginal', women are up for grabs. External persuasion across many cultures has been so powerful that this belief is difficult to resist and it reinforces our inner conviction that our bodies have no value.

Prostitute. Although many women would be utterly shocked if they were associated with prostitution, most of us have at some time exchanged sexual favours not for money, perhaps, but for something. We may have agreed to sex in anticipation of approval, promotion, affection, a quiet life, new living-room curtains or having the bathroom tap fixed. We also 'give' sex in return for financial security or to show appreciation for a meal or  being sympathetically treated, in return for advice and for company or friendship. It can be difficult to resist the pressure of believing that we *owe* it because of the assumption that sex always has a price.

Nymphomaniac. The crazed behaviour of this stereotype can subtly cause a lot of concern. Sometimes when we want to be more sexually expressive, enjoy ourselves more and acknowledge a sexual appetite, we can be struck by an inner fear that there is something a little degrading and shabby about feeling horny or making an explicit approach to a partner. This same fear extends to not making too much noise or appearing too earthy.

We can worry about being sexually greedy, or 'going over the top'. We can fear that our sexual needs will be seen as demeaning.

Eve. The image of the irresistible siren encourages us to see our bodies as powerful, not because of any inner quality but solely because of their external effect. Sometimes we can enjoy that power: knowing that someone is looking at us, wanting to touch us, that we are turning someone on, can be pleasurable. Being consciously seductive need not be harmful if both you and the other person are clear and trusting with each other. But this is often not the case.

Many women end up in situations that have gone much further than they intended and find it difficult to extricate themselves because they believe that they are responsible. Time and time again, women put up uncomplainingly with situations of sexual interference or harassment because they feel guilty or ashamed: being a woman can feel like a liability.

Slave. This is one of the most deeply believed stereotypes of female sexuality, written about in endless novels and porn. There are a few women who enjoy sexual masochism and humiliation in reality, but there are many more of us who are affected by the fantasy. Dependency on the man is undoubtedly suggested as well as gratitude for being made to submit and to suffer. This dependence can become an

addiction for some women so that they endure hurtful, abusive, rough or inconsiderate treatment from a partner but, because they believe they *need* that partner, they do not protest too loudly. In fact, they may even be persuaded that they enjoy such treatment because, after all, they believe they deserve it.

25

Superlay. This stereotype has a very damaging effect. It is not easy to say no or express reluctance to try some specific sexual activity or admit to a temporary lack of interest in sex when we believe that 'no' is a word which does not exist in Superlay's vocabulary. She instils in us a feeling of inadequacy. The mere fact that a woman can experience concern about the length of time taken to have an orgasm, whether or not it's the

right kind of orgasm, and whether she is responding in the right way in bed, is directly attributable to this stereotype.

Many of us worry about being ordinary or disappointing in comparison with a mythical ideal and, as a partner, we fear being clumsy or amateurish or being considered a sexual failure. Superlay also keeps us aware of the threat of competition from other women – we imagine that other women are 'better at it' and our dependence on our partners is strengthened.

The worst aspect of Superlay is that, unlike the others, she pretends to be something she isn't. While she pretends to encourage us to be sexually free and expressive and liberated, she is, in fact, robbing us completely of our spontaneity and further diminishing our natural capacity for sexual pleasure.

Black Widow. It is fairly easy to feed women's fears about castration. When an alarmist report spread wildly a couple of years ago suggesting that, because women were becoming more sexually responsive and assertive, men were suffering from an increase in problems of impotence, it was enough to make many women worry about the awful effect they might have on their partners if they dared to speak up in bed! From this model we learn to express our

sexual power and anger *indirectly*, so we use sex as a way to defuse a difficult situation, avoid criticism or confrontation, divert a man's anger or regain approval. Also, we use it as an indirect means of getting even: for example, withholding sex as a punishment. This model further encourages us to be alternately frightened of the symbol of the penis and contemptuous of it – to be intimidated by male sexuality and to dismiss men as mere studs.

Marauding Dyke. This caricature of a 'masculine' woman negates the image of strong active female sexuality which is independent of a male presence and affects both heterosexual and homosexual women. It can make it difficult for a woman to see herself as lesbian and feminine or to be able to make an approach to a woman she is attracted to without seeing it in terms of conquest.

Tragic Misfit. It is difficult to escape the power of this sad and failed image. Even the existence of gay counselling agencies risks reinforcing the suspicion that 'gay' means 'sick' or 'misguided' instead of confronting the public with the fact that it is conflict with a hostile culture which causes unhappiness, not the fact of being a woman who loves another woman.

Superdyke. This aggressive stereotype can be extended to include any woman who takes political action or makes a visible protest. She will run the risk of being totally discredited as a troublemaker, and a lesbian in the same breath. For some gay women, this stereotype can lead to a conflict between ideology and sexuality.

In seeking a model for a sexual relationship which entirely rejects the heterosexual partner, falling in love, enjoyment of penetration or experience of orgasm can feel inappropriate. Achieving an ideological ideal can feel incompatible with personal sexual needs and spontaneous expression.

These strong cultural images, the Virgin, the Whore and the Lesbian, affect us all as women whether we are in a relationship with a woman, a man or nobody at all. Between heterosexual women there is comparison and competition. They covertly assess and grade one another. Assessment depends on social status:

> She doesn't have any children so she can't understand.
> Has she *ever* been married?
> She must be a bit hard up to fall for him.
> Keep your eyes on your husband when she's around.
> Poor thing, she couldn't have any, you know.
> Well I know she's successful, but *look* at her children!

Pity, contempt, blame. And if loving other women means invisibility, doom, social ostracism, being unfeminine or anti-men, then attitudes towards gay women will be also tinged with pity, contempt and blame. Pity for the unfortunate lesbian who has her problems, poor dear, and couldn't make it with a man; contempt because she must have a terribly *boring* sex life; blame because she is doing a lot of harm to the struggle of ordinary women to be more liberated in their lives, getting ordinary women a bad name!

The view from the 'other side' is also coloured by those same feelings: pity for the unenlightened woman still trapped in her heterosexual married prison; contempt because she hasn't had the courage to break with the need for men's approval; blame because she is colluding with the enemy and is a traitor to real women.

It is ironic that so much comparison and division between women hinges on the opposite sex – whether present or absent, needed or rejected, approved or disapproved, included or excluded. What's more, our bickering reinforces the idea that a woman's validity and personal identity depend not on herself but on her *partner*.

If we were honest with each other, most of us would admit to experiencing a lot of confusion and uncertainty about our sexuality. Because this is uncomfortable we often feel the need to convince ourselves and others that we are living the *right* way.

We spend so much time and energy just trying to live up to or avoid certain stereotypes that we rarely make an opportunity to sort out what we want from what we feel is expected.

If you've ever felt confused, you could begin by reviewing your own individual history – your parents, family, religion, class, culture, education, your personal experience as a child, as an adolescent and as an adult. This will reveal a whole assortment of messages about female sexuality, male sexuality, masturbation, menstruation, female genitals, sexual behaviour – a mixture of 'do's and don'ts' which you have absorbed from your environment. Some may be recognizable from the familiar stereotypes, others may be more personal. Some will be easy to dismiss as ridiculous; others will be difficult to shake off.

One of the fascinating experiences in a group context is the exchange of messages. It's interesting to see the range of agreement and contradiction. Recognition is a first step – change, of course, is harder. I persistently have to remind myself that I don't have to have an orgasm in three minutes flat, that it's all right to be sexually greedy at times and that it's not the end of the world if I go off sex completely for weeks at a time. But still those little messages gnaw away, prompting me to feel inadequate or grotesque or a total sexual wash-out!

Change takes time and encouragement. It is important to establish an alternative – one which offers a view of a woman's sexuality as positive and not dependent upon any outside agent, a power which each woman can find within herself. Being open is the key – open to new learning and new information and open to looking at your body with new eyes.

Following on

1. One way of identifying your personal messages is to begin with a large blank piece of paper. Just let your mind wander back to your past and write down the name of the first person who comes into your head. Draw a box around the name and then write down, if you can, the specific message or messages you associate with that person. When you have finished, you'll probably find another person – a parent, friend, relative – you may think of a particular event in your life or a longer-term influence like school or a sexual relationship. Whatever comes to mind, write down the name and associated message. Messages may have been spoken or just conveyed by someone's attitude. Memories soon begin to flood back and often continue for a couple of days afterwards. It doesn't matter how

ludicrous the message sounds, write each one down. When you have finished, see what kind of picture your messages present. Do you find they say the same thing or do you find a lot of contradiction? Can you identify some which are no longer important to you while others still influence your attitudes today?

2. You may choose to share this exercise with one or more people who have written down some of their own messages.

3. Select one or two messages which are particularly powerful and find a positive contradiction. For example:

    Sex interferes with daily performance . . . Sex makes me feel dynamic and energized.

    Masturbation is wrong . . . Masturbation is natural.

    Homosexuals are frightening . . . I am a warm and loving lesbian woman.

    It's dangerous to be sexually attractive . . . I can enjoy being attractive without feeling guilty.

Write your positive messages down and display them where you will see them often so they can serve as a regular reminder!

4

Body Image

Watching a baby of a few months old, it is marvellous to see the pleasure it takes in its own body: totally at ease, uninhibited and completely without self-consciousness. Five or six years later this will have disappeared. By then, most children will be conscious of reacting to others' reactions and they will also be aware of the difference between genders. In general, boys will be physically encouraged towards action and strength whereas girls will learn very early that a key responsibility in having a female body is to present it as attractively as possible. This theme of decoration is not restricted to the West, although the yardstick of attractiveness will depend on the ideal in any particular culture. Value may be assessed on the colour of hair, width of hips or darkness of skin. Values may vary: slim is preferred in wealthier societies and fat is considered more prestigious in poorer ones. But whatever the measure, it is a *woman*'s body which has a rateable value.

Long before puberty most of us are aware of the importance and the significance of our appearance. Although we may individually rebel against the pressure to conform, we still know that girls are expected to be graceful, stay clean and avoid boisterous games. We learn through imitation and correction what brings us approval or rejection. We learn from school, if not before, that fatness and hairiness are undesirable. Exposure to the media makes it clear that physical beauty is the powerful magnet which draws the hero to fall in love with the heroine. This sequence provides us with the major clue as to why all these restrictions are necessary: being judged attractive is the passport to the altar and cradle.

We discover then that we have a second value: function. Our decorative potential is closely linked with our function as potential childbearers. We learn the dual importance of how our bodies should *look* and how our bodies should *work*. For maximum value they have to operate together – when women's bodies cease to have functional value with advancing years, they lose their decorative value as well. What do women look forward to in return? If we fulfil our decorative and functional roles, we anticipate acceptance, approval, admiration, love, security and a sense of power and importance.

The trouble is that for the human female the story doesn't end with attracting a mate and bearing offspring, as it does for other species. The attractive and functional potential of her body has become a blueprint for her personality, her behaviour and her interaction with other people. Many of us will have learned from an early age that attractiveness is not limited to what we look like, but applies equally to our behaviour: being obedient, gentle and compassionate is 'attractive'; being angry, outspoken or selfish is 'ugly'. Looking pretty is embodied in a smile not a scowl. Similarly, women are expected not only to bear and nurture their children, but also to extend their 'maternal' qualities – care, nurture, self-sacrifice – to one and all.

Some women are content with their role but many feel frustrated. The message is obvious: if you have a woman's body, you will grow up to be a woman. Our future role and value depends on our bodies. Therefore, our attitude to our bodies will reflect our feelings about being women. A woman's body image becomes the most fundamental part of her self-image. From menstruation to menopause, her self-image will change as her body image changes, for better or worse, depending on how she perceives the reactions of others. This parallel affects her all her life. If a woman's body is negated, she is negated; if her body is an object, she is an object; if her body is exploitable, she is exploitable; if her body is pleasing, she is pleasing; if her body has no value, she has no value.

Anticipation of an adult woman's status will depend on a young girl's view of her particular environment. Some women remember negative impressions from their past – they saw women as tired, doing the 'shit work', having no real power to make decisions, no ambition, being stuck, suffering and rarely protesting openly. Many women also remember their own mothers' ambivalence to their bodies and their sexuality – a double message as women hid or flaunted their bodies for effect. They could see the latter pleased men and made them want to touch them but were confused when those same bodies were treated with contempt. They saw their mothers endure their lives out of love for a man or men – her husband and/or her sons. If women favour men over other women, then is it because men are somehow better? It is certainly difficult for women not to gain the impression that a male *body* is preferable. People say that the male body is intrinsically faster, stronger, more active, while the female body is rounder, fatter, weaker and slower. Physiological facts – that women have smaller brains or less muscle mass – foster discriminatory attitudes at home and school. Smaller brains 'indicate' that women are less intellectual and less muscle mass that women are weaker. So women are considered dependent on the superior intellect and strength of men. While boys' physical and mental potential is encouraged to blossom, the physical and intellectual potential of girls is often left to wither on the stem. With so much evidence of comparative inferiority, it is meagre compensation that women can claim first prize for wider hips and the capacity for a longer (if stunted) lifespan!

Cast your mind back. Can you remember your reaction to puberty? Did you react with dismay? Delight? Indifference? Confusion? Do you remember your breasts beginning to bloom? Your first bra? I remember when my mother finally relented in the face of my persistent complaints about being the odd one out, and bought me an A-cup which I couldn't quite fill. I immediately locked myself away and tried on everything I could lay my hands on, inspecting my new profile in the mirror. My pride in those two bumps was rooted in my tender conviction that reaching adult womanhood would confer on me all the significance and love I would need.

Do you remember your own experience? What did you feel? Pride? Shame? Discomfort? Self-consciousness that your breasts were too small or too big? Smug or embarrassed if you developed earlier than others or mortified if you had to wait to catch everyone up? How did others respond? Where you teased or ostracized? Did you become aware that boys looked at you with a different interest? Did your father's attitude change? We learn early that our breasts are of special interest and significance to men because they often attract attention and comments. These internal changes and external reactions reinforce our decorative role. With menstruation we also become acutely aware of our functional role. Can you remember your reaction to this event? Were you proud because you felt you had 'arrived'? Or shocked because you were totally unprepared? Were you informed beforehand by your mother? Your father? Older sister?

No one at all? Was there a practical focus with instructions for washing or disposal? A warning about pregnancy or no mention at all of sexuality? Do you remember feeling a sense of embarrassment about the whole event? One woman, a mother who described buying a silver pendant well in advance to give to her daughter when the day finally came, showed an exceptional attitude as very few women remember it as an occasion for open celebration.

Our impressions and observations are important. If we see little or no personal pride and joy among the adult women in our immediate environment, we can feel ambivalent towards our growing bodies and what it means to be a woman. This ambivalence can turn to disillusionment as women become more and more aware of the reality of having a woman's body in this culture.

Woman as ornament. We see our bodies displayed to add decorative appeal to whatever is for sale – cream cakes, soap powder, car accessories. We get used to seeing women's bodies as objects along with other objects. In our consumer society, the outside appearance of the object is paramount, so the crucial question women automatically ask themselves is not 'Who am I?' but *'How do I look?'* It is difficult for many women to hold on to a sense of being a person, or to feel a sense of pride in their bodies in the face of this cultural obsession. They can no longer believe that this is a tribute to a woman's basic beauty and feel uncomfortable, vulnerable or angry.

Like any other objects, women's bodies can also be taken apart. Attractiveness is rated in parts: a woman's breasts, face, legs, hands, eyes, lips, buttocks are singled out for display. It is common sense that when you take any object to pieces it doesn't function and this again highlights the difficulty in retaining integrity and wholeness. If women hear a comment or joke about another woman's body – the size of her breasts or the shape of her legs – they more often hear mockery than respect. We may feel relief that for the moment it is someone else's body under review, but blatant assessment or ridicule undermines our own sense of pride and personal value.

Woman as vehicle. If we feel uncertain about our decorative value, can we expect more credibility from our functional role? It's hard to believe that giving birth is the high point of a woman's physical existence when most women are reduced to the status of patient during pregnancy and labour. Credibility is diminished when, at the precise moment that a woman's body should finally come into its own, she is often strapped up, tied down, drugged, immobile, helpless and totally without control over this one event for which she understood her body to be specially destined. Again, her body remains an object, but this time in a medical context.

Although pregnancy and childbirth tend to crystallize attitudes towards a woman's function, scarcely an opportunity is lost to drive home the message that women are expected to suffer. Eve must still be punished. The pains of labour are a continued reminder of her badness and so, by extension, is any pain associated with her function. Countless women seek help for painful periods and are told it is only to be expected. Time and time again a woman's pain is not taken seriously but dismissed as hysterical or neurotic. And because she is used to being considered an object, she will collude and endure the pain: it is impossible to fight outside battles effectively when *inside* she is still persuaded that suffering is her due.

Apart from a few flowers and cards at the time, women who are mothers don't usually find their personal status genuinely increased. In fact, women who have young children can find themselves positively unwelcome with a pushchair in public places and in Britain, which has fewer crèche facilities than any other country in Europe, women find it difficult to get help with childcare so they can take time for themselves. In the context of paid employment, the possibility of motherhood is considered a nuisance – a woman's potential for having and caring for children is actually a mark against her and often proves to be an insurmountable block to professional promotion. And, far from being rewarded for having children, women who have many children and are poor find themselves denied contraceptive or financial aid.

Even those women who make a conscious decision to have children because of personal enjoyment and fulfilment still find themselves having to face negative attitudes among medical personnel and often have to struggle to be treated as people, not impersonalized machines. Where then is the glory of motherhood? In reality, our function is about as much celebrated and admired as we celebrate and admire the oven whence comes the bun after baking.

Some women consider their bodies to be attractive and many women gain enormous joy from being mothers; but this doesn't change our awareness of the double message. With the female form revered and debased at the same time, and with motherhood theoretically encouraged but practically ignored, many of us experience a conflict within ourselves. This conflict shows itself in our thoughts, our feelings and our bodies. Sometimes this emerges as a chronic pattern in our lives, for example, of constant restlessness and tension or a desperate compulsion to try harder all the time; sometimes it is more acute, often occurring as depression and despair around the time of menstruation or after childbirth or during menopause. Because we do not see things in perspective we tend to direct our frustration towards what we believe to be the source of dissatisfaction. This can be a partner or child whose presence will often appear to be the cause of all our problems. But most of the time it is directed towards our bodies: *we blame our bodies as we blame ourselves.*

We do this in a variety of ways. Are any familiar to you?

Pulling ourselves to pieces. Most women find fault with their bodies. Catching sight of our reflections, what we see is not a single, whole entity but a collection of parts. At a conscious level, we can easily point to inadequacies in the way we look:

I don't like my nose.
I wish my breasts didn't sag.
If only my eyes were wider apart.
I don't know how to get rid of my flabby thighs?
I can't show my legs at my age.
You can't wear trousers with a behind like mine.

It's true that we may be responding to a direct criticism from someone else, but more often the criticism comes from inside our heads. Even if someone reassures us that we're not fat or that we look fine in a particular garment, we can still dismiss these reassurances because, inside, we're convinced that our own perception is the true one.

It's such an automatic process that we sometimes forget to ask ourselves too big/flat/short, for *whom*? Having learned the need for attractive parts, we compare these fragments to external media models, usually without any specific person in mind, and we rate ourselves in fragments, against some internal ideal.

Competition and pretence. There is not one single part which escapes comparative scrutiny (see diagram). Comparison with ideal and manufactured women encourages comparison and competition between real women. We watch other women squeezing themselves into unnatural shapes and camouflaging recalcitrant parts which won't conform despite any amount of effort. Women remove hair which offends and disguise their smell, colour and shape to such an extent that most women, given the heterosexual nature of their relationships, rarely have the opportunity to look at other women's bodies as they really are. Women are often the first to object to another woman who doesn't seem to be playing the same rules. A large woman in a bikini on the beach is likely to be the target of outrage from other women. What *does* she think she looks like?

how do you rate in the MEDIA MODEL attractiveness test? ☑

who - ME?

EYES
too: Wide ☐
Narrow ☐
Small ☐
Close ☐

CHEEKS
Too blotchy? ☐

HAIR
too: ☐ Lank
☐ Drab
☐ Frizzy

TEETH
too: Uneven? ☐ Stained ☐

NOSE
too: ☐ Large
☐ Small

CHIN
Too many of them? ☐

MOUTH
too: ☐ Thin
☐ Lips too uneven

ARMPITS
Too Hairy? ☐

SKIN
too: Red ☐
Dark ☐
Pale ☐
Wrinkled ☐

SHOULDERS
too: ☐ Boney?
☐ Square
☐ Masculine

UPPER ARMS
too: Flabby ☐
Muscular ☐

BREASTS
too ☐ Large
☐ Flabby
☐ Sagging
☐ Small

LOWER ARMS
☐ too Hairy?

BACK
too: Freckled ☐
Spotty ☐
Curved ☐
Muscular ☐

STOMACH
☐ too many bulges?

NAILS too:
☐ Square
☐ Crooked

BUTTOCKS
too:
☐ Round
☐ Big
☐ Fat

GENITALS
too:
☐ Hairy
☐ Smelly

HANDS too:
☐ Big
☐ Rough
☐ Red
☐ Unkempt

KNEES
☐ too Boney?

THIGHS
too:
☐ Crépey
☐ Bulging

LEGS
too: Hairy ☐
Crooked ☐

ANKLES
☐ too Thick

CALVES
too:
☐ Muscular
☐ Veined
☐ Shapeless

FEET
☐ too Big?

Rejection and fear. It is we who cannot accept the truth about our bodies without feeling uncomfortable. Small wonder that natural hair, sweat, fat and roundness are discouraged. It seems that in the more westernized cultures, flat has more appeal than curved, neat and trim more appeal than full and round, hard muscle more than soft fat, linear more than circular – so natural is rejected.

Some women express a sense of fear about their bodies. The parts which carry more female associations – breasts, softness, bellies – are unacceptable, which suggests a deep-rooted fear that the body (loose flesh) has the potential to overwhelm and therefore must be held in check (tight muscle). They prefer the muscular parts of their bodies to the fleshier parts. It is important to remember that when we reject certain parts, we can cut off their sensation as well because we cannot allow ourselves to trust or receive pleasure through them. Numbness, like extreme fatness, can provide a protective barrier against our true feelings.

Punishment. Another pattern you may recognize is trying to lick the offending object into shape! We punish our bodies by wearing extra-tight clothing which restricts the flow of blood or air and we wear clothes which restrict movement of the legs or spine in an attempt to present ourselves more decoratively. Many women use punishing diets to lose unwanted pounds to prove they are still in control. We overeat and undereat in an attempt to resolve the internal conflict, and consequently our bodies suffer. Some women even resort to drastic measures of surgery so that the offending bulge or wrinkle or fold will be banished for ever! But none of these punishments removes the internal blame.

Apart from these short-term punishments, we are familiar with the longer-term version: continued subjection of our bodies to excessive work and stress so that they are eventually subdued by fatigue and exhaustion, illness, even death. This form of punishment is invisible and is the most insidious because it attracts most social approval: 'She works *so* hard, I don't know how she does it!' We find it difficult to call a halt voluntarily, so we go on until we are *forced* to stop by being laid out flat with a virus or a slipped disc. Even in the knowledge of women's greater powers of endurance, we push ourselves to ludicrous and debilitating lengths.

We fail to set physical limits or social limits. By punishing our bodies, we punish ourselves. If it all gets too much, we can always go into hiding. We can wash our hands of the whole problem and disown our bodies completely. Some women refuse to learn anything about their bodies. 'I'm *completely* ignorant about my body,' they say with childlike pride, leaving it up to partners or doctors to take responsibility. This attitude risks total detachment from everything our bodies are telling us. Letting ourselves go is fine if it means shedding inhibition but can be disastrous if it means abandoning any respect for or interest in our bodies.

A common denominator among women in many parts of the world is a lack of *inner* self-esteem based on this lack of *physical* self-esteem. We are often slow to confront verbal abuse, physical abuse and sexual abuse because we lack this fundamental sense of beauty and worth in our own right. And, try as we may, we cannot earn it from anyone on the outside. It has to come from the inside.

Imagine something you prized, which you thought beautiful, unique and essential to your life: imagine your reaction if someone handled that prize with callousness or dishonour or violence. Probably immediate outrage – a 'no' which would erupt from deep within, born of a fierce sense of belonging and passion.

To touch this pride and passion we have an obvious starting point: our bodies. We have to learn about them, re-acquaint ourselves with them, see the truth instead of a distorted image. We have to look at the mirror within, not the external mirror which is warped by our dependence on the reflection.

Looking is the first exercise that class participants are asked to do at home after the first session. As you might imagine, everyone feels an enormous resistance! Standing naked in front of a full-length mirror and really looking at yourself can be an overwhelming experience. We are used to seeing our faces but we tend not to give our bodies more than a fleeting or disparaging glance when getting out of the bath, and although we may be used to undressing for a lover or doctor or perhaps for an artist or on the beach, we rarely do it for ourselves.

The resistance produces all sorts of excuses for not doing the exercise. You may find similar excuses: too cold, too hot, too busy, inundated with visiting relations, no mirror, no lock on the door, kids interfering. You may find yourself saying you don't see the point. Full guidelines for the exercise are given below, but it can be helpful to know what to expect. As you stand there listening to your thoughts while you face your naked image, you will probably feel vulnerable. This will trigger past associations and experiences and many messages about *parts* of your body. There are often feelings associated with those parts: sadness at loss of youthful quality; pride at legs which were called attractive; revulsion at the heavy belly.

This process can evoke deep feelings. One woman in the group had dismissed her breasts because they had gone droopy after breast-feeding two children. Instead of pretending that her breasts didn't exist, she was now able to come to terms with their change of appearance as marking a stage in her life, to acknowledge her regret and see her breasts as the insignia of motherhood. Another took a long time to come to terms with her caesarian scar, which reminded her always of her 'failure' to give birth the 'proper' way. It took a lot of courage for her to continue looking and accepting, but she did so. Another woman felt her legs were hideously hairy and couldn't bear to look at them; she too came to accept them as part of her whole body and the dread of anyone else seeing them gradually diminished. Seeing is always the first step towards loving.

Following on

1. If you would like to try the exercise described above , you will need a warm comfortable room, a mirror (preferably full-length),

at least half an hour with a guarantee of no interruptions and the motivation! This is a personal and private experience so you should be on your own. You can set the scene by lighting a candle or playing some favourite music – anything which you feel will contribute to a pleasurable and relaxed mood. As you look, you may begin by seeing your body in parts. If you do, notice any associations or 'judgements' which come to mind. Use the questions below to take you through the process:

a) What parts of your body do you most enjoy looking at? What do you like about them?

b) Which parts of your body give comfort and pleasure to others? Which parts give you pleasure and comfort? In what ways?

c) Which parts of your body do you enjoy looking at least? What is it about them? How do those parts feel when they are touched?

d) What do you enjoy about your body as a whole? What sort of emotions do you associate with different parts of your body?

e) Notice how you feel during the exercise, e.g. curious, inhibited, interested, impatient, sad, anxious, wondering why you haven't done this before.

2. You may like to write down the answers to these questions and any other thoughts or observations that occur to you.

3. When you have finished looking, take time to get to know your body through touch. Imagine you are looking and touching with the eyes of a child – feel the different textures and contours as if for the first time. Vary firm strokes with gentle strokes. Notice what touch and where feels pleasurable, irritating, neutral or erotic.

4. Repeat 1 and 2 on another occasion. At different times and in different moods we see and feel our bodies differently. If you feel unhappy you are likely to be more critical, and if you feel content you will probably take pleasure in your body.

5. Find a way to get back in touch with your body through some physical exercise, like running or dancing or swimming. Choose an activity you can enjoy for its own sake rather than one which has a goal.

6. I know from experience how difficult this is, but the benefits to be gained from disciplining yourself to take at least fifteen minutes' relaxation a day are unlimited: yoga, meditation, going for a walk,

lying down and breathing deeply – any relaxation exercise will help.

7. Another way to get to know your body is by keeping a menstrual calendar. You can note how your appetite, your mood, your dreams, your intellectual, sexual and emotional energies fluctuate each month. If you have spent a long time being defensive about these changes in order to resist being put down, then it may seem strange to adopt such an open and direct approach, but you can reinstate them *positively* into your life.

8. If you find that one or two parts of your body have come in for a lot of criticism (from yourself or others), you might like to find some positive way of cherishing those parts so that you can begin to accept the whole of you. Being lovingly massaged is one good way.

A Rose by Any Other Name

There is a fair chance that even if you complete the exercise described in the last chapter and look carefully at your whole body, there will be one fragment which you overlook. Unless you adopted a highly unusual pose in front of the mirror, your genitals will have remained hidden from view! It is a part of our bodies which we look at least, have least knowledge of and, often, least affection for.

When participants in a class are asked to look at their genitals at home, the responses will often reflect their surprise:

I've never really given it much thought although I've let hundreds of doctors prod me around.

I never thought of looking myself.

I haven't looked since I was a kid and a friend and I used to do it together in secret.

I looked once when I got an infection but I wouldn't think of looking otherwise.

Some women have looked before because they were curious and wanted to check themselves out, but even this part of our anatomy doesn't escape comparison with a mythical ideal so women sometimes think they are deformed and are frightened by the experience. Even those who've done it once in a self-help group insist there can't be any point in doing it a second time! Many are simply horrified by the prospect of looking, without really understanding why.

As well as being shrouded in pubic hair, a woman's genitals are shrouded in ambiguity. I remember once admiring the beauty of a rose with a friend. We exclaimed at the depth of the colour, the velvety petals, the shape of the flower, both of us sharing its simple yet profound beauty until, that is, I remarked that the shape was evocative of a woman's genitals. Immediately my friend grimaced, 'Do you *have* to?' he said, adding that my comparison had spoiled his enjoyment completely.

Distaste just about sums up the general attitude of most men and, by extension, most women to this particular part of a woman's anatomy. Women often disassociate themselves from this part because, although it is only one of many fragments, it is the one which has come to symbolize female sexuality most precisely. Attitudes are affected by cultural messages and personal associations.

Do you remember learning by implication that this part of your body was different from the rest? Being told as a child not to touch, or to wash 'there' with a separate cloth? That a girl's legs should be kept together so that nobody can see up her dress? When you realized that your 'thing' was different from a boy's 'thing', did you feel equally proud of yours or did you feel you had something *missing*?

With menstruation, any covert difference becomes officially acknowledged. And when adolescent gropes begin around the breasts, the hands will descend sooner or later towards the crotch, as if drawn by some magnetic force. Whatever 'it' is down there, the boys certainly seem to want it. The boys may change to men but the message remains unchanged. We learn that we have a powerful little something between our legs but 'it' remains mysterious. Apart from the memory of doctor-and-nurse games, we often grow up completely unaware of what this powerful little something looks like.

This is reinforced by the cultural view – it is either totally eclipsed or totally exposed.

Eclipsed. Discouraged from showing an interest in our own genitals, the reality of female anatomy means we are not going to get a very clear picture from seeing other women's bodies in the flesh or on canvas or in stone. And not only is there no picture, there is no name. Vague terms like

Down there
Privates
Crotch
It
She/her
Rude bits

Sex
Waterworks
Between your legs
Bottom

reinforce the mystery and confusion.

Exposed. With exposure, we find a wider range of words, more specific ones which refer crudely to basic physiology, and we learn there is hair:

Pussy
Beaver
Muff
Bush
Guinea pig
Man-trap
Crack.

With visual exposure in pornographic imagery, we find the enigma replaced by a grotesque display of specific detail, like a butterfly in a case, its wings spread out for all to see but its body robbed of life by a pin.

Whether covered up or exhibited it is difficult to avoid the association of shame and, although we may try to hide our ears to it, we cannot ignore the word 'cunt'. Nor does it escape our notice that in many languages 'cunt' is used to describe an object of *utter* revilement and contempt.

We may feel slightly or extremely uncomfortable with these words. Clinical words like vulva or genitals or vagina (which is anatomically misleading) can make our bodies seem very distant. Some of us use more neutral words like 'fanny'. In a tiny attempt to counteract the contempt associated with it, I like to use the word cunt with a positive tone in its literal context, but I know that it will take a very long time before women can see it written or hear it spoken without feeling it is offensive and impossible for them to use.

Whatever your feelings, it is important to find *some* word even if you make up your own. There are a few positive terms in existence – like 'yoni' which derives from the Hindu culture, or 'honeypot' to which I was first introduced by an Italian woman. You may have a pet name of your own or one that your partner uses. A name you can feel happy and comfortable with is what matters.

Naming our genitals for ourselves and looking for ourselves are two important steps in confronting the deeply negative and abusive connotations surrounding them. Many women don't look at their own genitals, many women are heterosexual and many women don't look at pornography: the result is that, as adults, we give partners and doctors access to a part of our bodies with which we are personally unfamiliar. The experience of looking at different women's genitals is informative and can defuse some of the general mystery and alarm. Studying a series of 'cunt slides' in a sexuality class gives us permission to look and our curiosity overcomes disgust or anxiety. Real information takes the place of silence and mystery, and the variations in colour, shape and size are a source of fascination as well as reassurance.

Nevertheless, unpleasant associations will also emerge: smell, mess, mis-shapen parts, slabs of meat, wounds, bloody, raw, open, vulnerable. Women have absorbed the cultural negativity and made it their own. Where does this shame and loathing come from? Originally from a very deep fear. The mystery surrounding a woman's ability to get pregnant and give birth was first compounded by early man's ignorance. With nothing visible on the outside, it was believed that a woman produced a baby through magic, so her body was viewed with a mixture of fearfulness and awe. When the connection between intercourse and conception was understood, innocent wonder gave way to envy and then fear. Although we pride ourselves on being sophisticated and living in a highly technological age, we can still see evidence of this fear and fascination. The current controversy about AID (artificial insemination by donor) illustrates a felt need to control and to exert scientific and legal pressure on this mysterious and miraculous power.

In the past this powerful process was never seen to be more threatening than during menstruation, when the vagina was believed to be at its most potent and evil. Again, despite a rational rejection of this belief, men in most cultures today feel a deep, emotional barrier against touching this part of a woman's body when she is menstruating, however 'clean' she may make herself. This extends to a general reservation felt by many men about touching this place with a hand or a mouth at any time at all.

Fear of female sexual power gave rise to myths about women whose vaginas had teeth which cut off the penis during copulation. This suggests that, for a man, heterosexual intercourse was akin to a spiritual kamikaze mission: he entered the vagina with his penis erect, strong and full of life; he would emerge from that same vagina, his penis limp, lifeless, spent. His spirit had been consumed. His spirit was dead. A fear of death is also reinforced by deeply buried memories of a woman's genitals during the struggle for life and birth. Our lives begin with a separation from life inside the womb, from total union with the mother. Separation is an ending and thus a kind of death.

Association with spiritual death, which has recurred in mythology and imagery (remember also the Black Widow), is still evident in modern society's treatment of women's genitals. This doesn't happen by chance. Since a woman's genitals represent the core of her sexual and maternal power, this part of her body is selected as a symbolic and literal object of abuse. The image of death is ever-present but this time it is the woman, not the man, who dies. Part of a woman's spirit dies when her labia are drawn back in pornographic exhibition; it dies every time her vagina is penetrated with violence and hate; it dies every time her clitoris is ritually mutilated; it dies every time her vulva, in the very act of giving birth, becomes the impersonal object of routine surgery.

The immense power of cultural negativity makes itself felt in all sorts of ways. Even without personal experience of physical violation, we can still be affected, consciously or unconsciously, by the acting out of this ancient fear. We often feel a deep sense of shame and lose touch with our sexual energy and power.

The very best way I know of confronting these feelings is to get to know this part ourselves. Because of the commitment to the group, women will take the time during the week to look at themselves when they might not otherwise have done so. Once over the anxiety and concern, most women report that it is a very positive experience:

After all my resistance I really got into it. I enjoyed it.
I loved the folds and crinkles.
I enjoyed the colour variations.
It felt like a beginning.
Once I forgot about the strangeness, I became quite absorbed in looking.
I saw a person in the lines, like a small fairy.
I saw a hooded figure, like a wise old woman.
I really didn't like what I saw and that made me very unhappy.
It's going to take me a long time to get to know my cunt.
I was fascinated to know what the other person sees when we make love.
The lips of mine were quite uneven.
Mine was like a huge rose.
Mine was like the folds in a long curtain!

·A Private View·

Exploration continues with 'mapping', a short but rewarding journey around one's genitals, this time to identify which bit is where. Even if you have some vague knowledge of the general layout, this exercise gives a lot of personally useful information. Some guidelines are given at the end of this chapter.

Later on in the course, women may wish to examine themselves with a speculum so that they can look inside as well as out. The remarkable view of the cervix inside the vagina shows that there is nothing to be afraid of or ashamed of – indeed, there is everything to be proud of. Doing this for the first time is often easier with someone else to hold the torch while you position the mirror and speculum, so we devote some time to doing this in class. It becomes an adventure of self-discovery with the support of interested and caring people. The experience is a high point: women who have given birth are amazed to see where their children actually came through; others check on scars or the position of a coil or how their cervix is affected by their menstrual cycle. Others are fascinated to see what happens inside other women as well! One woman, a doctor by profession, remarked that although she'd looked at hundreds of women's genitals in her work, she'd never actually *seen* one before that evening. After looking and learning, class participants are asked to make a drawing – not an anatomically correct diagram but a portrait because we usually think of a portrait as the picture of someone or something cherished and valued. All of this is part of a process of healing some of the abuse – both individual and general.

One of the most powerful and moving experiences for me in a class is when the portraits are displayed. Unlike the usually exhibited fragments, these pictures are seen in a context of tenderness and strength. Each woman looks at the others' portraits, in celebration not exploitation. We begin to reclaim individually and collectively the beauty of this eclipsed part of ourselves.

On one course was a religious woman whose way of celebrating this new discovery was unique and unforgettable. She told us that looking at her genitals during the week had made her cry, that for some reason it had evoked many memories of her mother and also of her own decision to become a nun. But, she said, as she began to draw, she felt a surge of love in her and joy in her sexuality. She told us that she had sung a hymn to her cunt, a sung prayer of celebration. I asked her if she would sing it again for all of us. As her lone voice rang out, tears came to everyone's eyes, tears of wonder at this woman who sang of her vulnerability and joy. It was a perfect gift to herself and to us all.

Following on

1. **Looking.** Follow the instructions for setting a warm and comfortable scene at the end of Chapter 4. You will need a mirror which stands on its own, a good light and a comfortable position, preferably with something behind your back to support you. Make sure you have arranged a time when you will be uninterrupted for at

least half an hour. Then take your time to become acquainted. Notice how you feel during this exercise: curious? anxious? interested? fascinated? See if an image or association comes to mind. Find a positive image for yourself.

2. **Mapping**. You can continue with the mapping exercise and identify the following:

Your clitoris. If you pull back the clitoral hood you will see the tip (or glans) more clearly. This will look pink and shiny. Trace back from the tip along the shaft. It will feel rubbery under your finger but as you move back and forth you may feel it begin to get bigger and harder. Feel for yourself the length of the clitoral shaft. Sometimes people think of the clitoris as referring only to the glans which is the most sensitive part. A woman has as many nerve endings in the glans of the clitoris as a man has in the glans of his penis. This explains why the tip can feel excruciatingly painful at times. Some women feel pleasure when it is touched only when they are highly aroused, others when they are not aroused, so find out for yourself.

Your labia. Distinguish the outer lips covered in hair from the inner lips which are the inside folds. Your own shape will be as unique as your face – one lip may be wider or longer than the other, the colour may vary from grey to pink to red, light to dark brown, very dark brown or a multi-coloured mixture! Stroke inside and out to feel where your lips are most sensitive.

Your urethra. Moving down you will see the opening to your vagina. As you move, stop to look at your urethra – through which urine passes. This opening is tiny and sometimes difficult to see but worth looking for.

Your vaginal opening. You will see the entrance, sometimes surrounded by little bits of pink tissue which don't have any sensation – these are vestiges of your hymen, which can be found about an inch in. Typically, there is little information about the hymen other than its symbolism. In fact, it is a thin membrane, rather like that around a hard-boiled egg, but it is flexible and easily broken, only occasionally needing surgical invervention to remove it.

Your p.c. muscle. As you sit, look at your vaginal entrance, imagine yourself in the middle of a pee and then having to stop suddenly. You will be able to see a movement around your vagina. This is part of a band of muscle called the pubococcygeal muscle (p.c. muscle for short) which stretches from your pubic bone to your coccyx or tail bone. Some women are introduced to it as the pelvic floor muscle when preparing for childbirth. This is the muscle which contracts

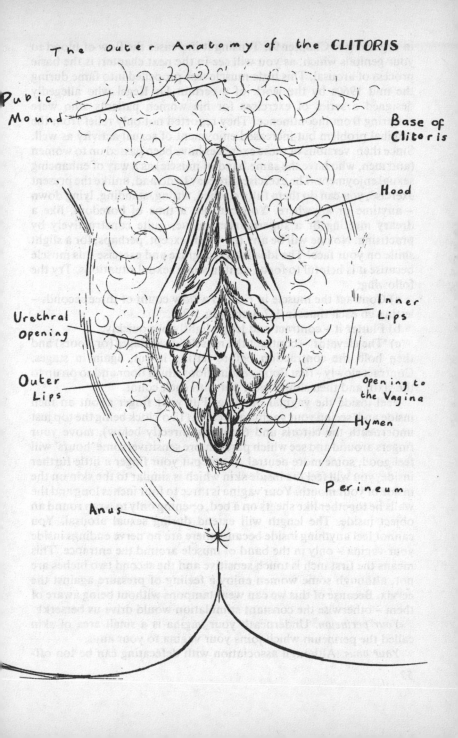

The Outer Anatomy of the CLITORIS

Pubic Mound

Base of Clitoris

Hood

Inner Lips

Urethral Opening

Outer Lips

Opening to the Vagina

Hymen

Perineum

Anus

in orgasm (see Chapter 9). Tensing it increases the flow of blood to your genitals which, as you will see in the next chapter, is the basic process of arousal. This little muscle was propelled into fame during the mid 1960s by the work of a certain Dr Kegel who allegedly designed a series of exercises for his women patients who were suffering from incontinence. They reported not only relief from the original problem but increased enjoyment of sexual activity as well. Since then, versions of these exercises have been passed on to women (and men, who have the same band of muscle) as a way of enhancing sexual enjoyment. The exercises are easy to do and, unlike the present exercise, you can do them fully clothed, sitting, standing, lying down – anytime or anywhere. You can use a time of boredom, like a dreary meeting or a supermarket queue, quite constructively by practising. No one will be any the wiser, except, perhaps, for a slight smile on your face! The idea is to recognize and exercise this muscle because it is helpful to focus on it in some sexual situations. Try the following:

a) Contract the muscle in time to a slow count of three seconds – letting go each time: in 1-2-3 and out 1-2-3.

b) Flutter it – contract and let go lightly but quickly.

c) 'The elevator' – contract the muscle in six stages (or floors) and then hold the contraction before letting it out, again in stages. Contract slowly – first floor, second floor, third floor and so on up to the sixth and then slowly let it out with each count.

Feel inside the vaginal opening. Put your finger about an inch inside and, seeing your vagina as a clock (12 o'clock being the top just underneath the clitoris and 6 o'clock directly below), move your fingers around and see which part is more sensitive; some 'hours' will feel good, some more neutral. If you put your finger a little further inside, you will feel the inside skin which is similar to the skin on the inside of your mouth. Your vagina is three to four inches long and the walls lie together like sheets on a bed, opening only to wrap round an object inside. The length will extend during sexual arousal. You cannot feel anything inside because there are no nerve endings inside your vagina – only in the band of muscle around the entrance. This means the first inch is touch sensitive and the second two inches are not, although some women enjoy a feeling of pressure against the cervix. Because of this we can wear tampons without being aware of them – otherwise the constant stimulation would drive us berserk!

Your perineum. Underneath your vagina is a small area of skin called the perineum which joins your vagina to your anus.

Your anus. Although association with defecating can be too off-putting for some people to consider that this part of their anatomy can be remotely pleasurable, there are many who find that they derive enormous erotic pleasure from anal stimulation.

There is obviously much more to our anatomy than this short exercise will reveal. There are some excellent and thorough books available, some of which are listed on pages 182–3.

3. **Portraits.** You may like to draw your own portrait. Don't worry about your ability to draw. It doesn't matter whether your drawing is an impression or more life-like. Decide whether you want to work within a small frame or on a large piece of paper, and whether or not you want to use colours. The important thing is to make the experience positive and pleasurable.

4. **Self-examination.** The following instructions are adapted from *Our Bodies, Ourselves* (see Further Reading on page 183). I have not included clinical information because this information is readily available in the books mentioned. If you want to explore further you will need extra equipment – namely, a plastic speculum and some KY jelly or similar lubricant, not vaseline. To see, you will need a strong directional light from a torch.

It's a good idea to have your own plastic speculum to prevent the transfer of infection. Wash it in plain soap and warm water after each use. Go through the motions of opening and locking the speculum before you actually examine yourself.

a) When you are familiar with the manipulation of the speculum, empty your bladder, position yourself comfortably, sitting or lying down with knees bent and feet placed wide apart. You may want to prop yourself up on a pillow.

b) Lubricate the speculum with a small amount of KY jelly. Holding the speculum closed, gently insert it sideways into your vagina, at the same angle you would a tampon.

c) When it is in all the way, slowly turn it so that the handle points upwards.

d) Then grasp the handle and firmly push the shorter, outside section of the handle towards you. This will open the blades of the speculum inside you. If you have not already heard a click, push down the outside section until you do. The speculum is then locked open.

e) If you have never done this before, or are in an awkward position, your vagina may try to reject the speculum. Also, you may have to move the speculum around or reinsert it before the cervix

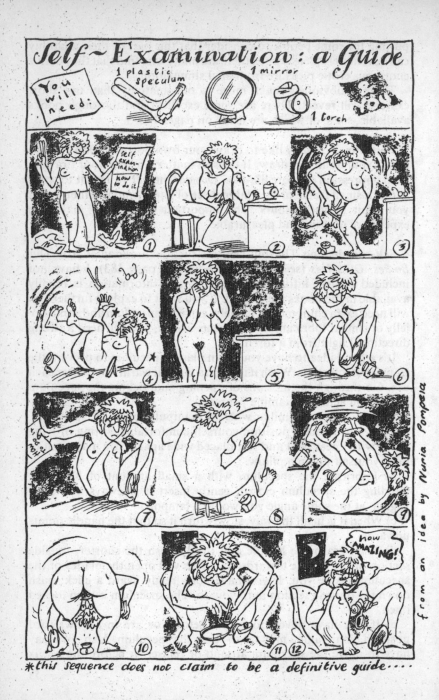

pops into view. A friend can be very helpful here, particularly if your cervix is off to one side (a common occurrence).

f) It is often easier to have the light pointed at the mirror and the mirror held so that you can see into the tunnel that your speculum has opened up. This pink area, which looks much like the walls of your throat, is your vagina. At the end of the tunnel is a pinkish, bulbous dome-shaped protrusion. This is your cervix. If you don't see it, then gently draw out the speculum and push down with your stomach muscles. This usually causes the cervix to pop into view.

g) To remove the speculum, *keep it open* and slowly pull it straight out. For information on obtaining a speculum see page 181.

6
Time for Oneself

One of the drawbacks to masturbation is the word itself. It has a ring of dullness about it and suggests something solemn and mechanical rather than light-hearted and fun. But in order to become more familiar with the sensations of our genitals, we have to consider the pros and cons of 'self-stimulation'. In most cultures today the subject remains completely unmentionable. In this culture, masturbation is acknowledged as a normal phase of sexual development but it is most often associated with adolescent boys. And even though in the last fifteen years sex therapy and sex research have endorsed masturbation for adult women, many still feel a deep reluctance.

One reason for this is a consequence of the ambivalence I described in the last chapter. When we see something beautiful, we reach out to touch it, so that with our fingers we can add another dimension to the beauty we see with our eyes. In the same way we recoil from the idea of touching something which is frightening or ugly. If touching our genitals feels disconcerting or unfamiliar, we are unlikely even to consider the prospect of self-stimulation or, if we try it once, anxiety will neutralize our ability to take any pleasure from the sensations.

Another reason for our reluctance is the general awareness of those cautionary tales about masturbation which exert a powerful influence over people's beliefs. Some of them are illustrated opposite. The oldest objections derive from religious doctrine. Since procreation was vital, sexual activity which wasted valuable semen, including coitus interruptus, was judged a sin. The fulminations of the churches still reverberate, producing a profound sense of guilt and the

conviction that self-indulgence is dangerous.

Physical cautions are more often associated with men because masturbation, like cricket or football, has traditionally been considered a male activity. For women, its association has remained rather obscure, apart from one graphic historical exception: as sexual desire was considered a male prerogative, autonomous female sexual desire was considered a symptom of insanity. Someone found what they considered to be an inspired solution: remove the clitoris and remove the source of all the trouble. So clitoridectomy, a kind of genital lobotomy, was used as a 'cure' until fifty years ago in Britain for women who exhibited these unfortunate symptoms.

The psycho-social disadvantages were developed by enlightened experts who, after studying human sexual behaviour, pronounced adult masturbation unhealthy: it was a narcissistic diversion from the true path of heterosexual fulfilment. It was also hinted that masturbation is addictive and can cause a person to forget how to relate to a partner. Small wonder that despite the apparent permission, many of us are still worried that masturbation is immature or inferior and just a fourth-rate substitute for the real thing. The power of these cautionary tales lies not in their truth but in our *belief* in their truth.

For women, particularly, the deepest resistance stems from our reluctance to experience any kind of sexual activity on our own. This is based on early experience. Many of us experience our first genital sensations through the action of a partner. In a society which permits pre-marital sex, many teenage girls agree to sex as a way of acquiring increased social status, ensuring the boy's love by accommodating his need. This pattern remains into adult life with the clear association between sensations of sexual pleasure and the skill or magical quality of a partner. This has become so deeply ingrained that we can believe that a partner *has* to be present for us to feel sexually aroused. In the face of this, masturbation can seem like trying to clap with one hand.

As a result, women become physically dependent on received information: information about our bodies comes through someone else's. At a deeper, emotional level, our sexual self-esteem leans heavily on the prop of reassurance from a sexual partner. This dependence makes us exceptionally vulnerable to a total sense of rejection if that other person should stop finding us interesting or desirable. The dependence is expressed in various ways which you may recognize: feeling grateful for someone's expressed attraction; feeling that life is empty unless we have a lover; feeling sexually attractive only as long as we have a partner who finds us sexually attractive; or hanging on to relationships because we do not want to be alone. So often we believe that *alone equals lonely*.

Even though literature about masturbation has been available for some time – encouraging many women to read and experiment successfully for themselves – there is still something missing. When masturbation has been promoted, it has usually either been touted as a prelude to the main event or therapeutically recommended as a more efficient way of reaching orgasm. But with orgasm achieved, comes the full stop. Permission to masturbate hasn't proved to be the solution to a general dissatisfaction with or confusion about sexual relationships. The deeper significance of masturbation for women has been lost.

The importance of masturbation is the quality of time spent with oneself. It provides a woman with an opportunity to step out of her various roles and responsibilities and outside definitions and be intimate with herself. Like walking, prayer, meditation, it is a way of being with yourself. But it is a physical way which specifically includes the sexual part and can be confronting, healing, nourishing, energizing, relaxing or releasing – any and all of these depending on your particular need at the time. This is why it is relevant to a woman's sexuality as a whole part of her life.

In a group, women share their earliest memories of self-pleasuring – many remember playing in the bath or with a certain soft toy or climbing ropes in the gym. They remember pleasure, sometimes guilt, knowing it was a secret and that somehow it was 'wrong'. Sometimes they were found out, sometimes punished. Some women discover masturbation much later in adult life, others never masturbate at all. There isn't a norm – the important part of the discussion is to share our views. You may find your own view included in these examples:

I've never thought about it.
I used to do it as a child but never since.
I read about it when I was in my mid-twenties so I just tried it!
I've tried but I don't get any pleasure out of it.
I don't get anywhere.
It's fun.
I do it when I want to comfort myself.
I have done it sometimes but now I'm in a relationship, I don't have to.
It just makes me feel dissatisfied.
Never!
It's an important part of knowing myself.

Many women find masturbation a positive experience for all sorts of reasons:

It's a good way to learn your own responses.
It's a good way to experiment.
You don't have to take care of anyone else.
You can fantasize exactly what you want.
You can take it with you wherever you go.
It's cheap.
You can't get pregnant.
It's fun.
It's a celebration.
It's healing.
It's sexual relief.
It's good when you're bored/horny/irritated/tense . . .

and it comes highly recommended as a remedy for insomnia, menstrual pain, headaches, fatigue and backache!

Far from being a heavy mechanical grind, masturbation can be a creative way of being a lover to yourself. Some women in the group will share the details of their experience:

I use a shower attachment when I'm lying in a hot bath and run the water up and down my cunt until I come with a splash!

I was given a vibrator for my birthday which is very stimulating. I have to use a soft cloth between me and it – but it's great fun.

Sometimes I make a whole ritual of it: I have a long bath, then I put body lotion all over my body afterwards and I lie down with a glass of wine and some music and there I am, relaxed and enjoying my body. Sometimes I go on to stimulate my clitoris but sometimes I just enjoy it, without an orgasm.

Sometimes when I'm busy doing something else, I suddenly get a 'clit call'. I usually go and lie down on my back and spread my legs and I stroke all over my breasts and stomach but concentrate around and on my clitoris.

Lying on our fronts or backs, in the security of a bed or the boldness of the open air, on trains or planes, sometimes the most extraordinary places – anywhere is possible! Some women enjoy something inside their vaginas as well as stimulation outside – hairbrush handles, candles, even carrots wrapped in clingfilm are among all sorts of ingenious suggestions for extra enjoyment.

Masturbation doesn't take over from sex with a partner. It is something else completely. This is why women sometimes feel masturbation is a secret, quite apart from a relationship. Other women feel it is part of a sexual relationship as well. This doesn't mean that your partner 'does' it for you, but that you stimulate yourself. This can be part of making love together but there is another option: simply taking the time for yourself alone while your partner holds you or lies with you. If your partner is turned on you may find this a help or a hindrance, but it does require trust. To give yourself permission to get absorbed in your body while someone else is there means flying in the face of so many messages about selfishness and passivity that it will require a very deep trust in that other person. But it can be a very enriching experience to share together.

There need be no goals or norms in masturbation. But this kind of time spent on our own can teach us the importance of certainty, care and choice. Certainty is the ability to know and trust our bodies, to be familiar and at ease with their sensations and to allow ourselves to let go. Care is the intention to pleasure rather than punish, to cherish rather than dismiss. Choice is the freedom to stop or change in response to inner signals rather than push ourselves towards fulfilling expectations or goals.

Following on

1. If you want to clarify your own attitudes to masturbation, you could answer the following questions:

a) What are your earliest memories about self-pleasuring? What did you feel about it then?

b) How do you feel now about masturbation?

c) What is your current pattern? When? How? Have you ever experimented with sexual toys?

d) Have you ever shared masturbation with a partner? If so, what was your experience? If not, why not?

2. It is useful and rewarding to answer the above questions with others and to share your feelings and ideas.

3. You could consider trying something different for yourself – taking

a long pleasurable time, perhaps, or buying a vibrator (information on page 181).

7

Arousal

Sexual activity can be a time of intense and absorbing pleasure, but many women and their lovers do not understand the process of pleasure and arousal and what affects their experience of their bodies during sexual activity. When things don't work out as we want, many of us are confused and this makes communication almost impossible – if we don't know for ourselves, we cannot clearly tell someone else.

'Arousal' is an umbrella term which describes a pattern of changes affecting our bodies and minds simultaneously. Leave behind the clinical diagrams for a moment and imagine instead a large surface of slow-moving water, with a gentle current directing it towards the distant brim of a waterfall. The water moves towards it, is pulled towards the edge, gathering momentum as it nears the fall. The current is stronger and the movement faster. As it nears the edge the sound of the rushing water is deafening – no other sound can be heard. On and on the water moves until suddenly it falls over the edge, cascading freely into a pool below where the movement gradually subsides and disperses.

Sexual arousal is best understood by looking first at what happens to our bodies and then at what happens in our minds even though, in reality, they are all part of the same complex chain of interdependent responses.

Sexual arousal is triggered by a stimulus which prompts the brain to set in motion a number of reflex responses, causing a sequence of physiological changes. These include an increase of the blood flow into the abdomen and pelvic area due to the extra activity of the heart which quickens the pulse and raises the pressure of the blood passing through the body. The original stimulus can be physical or psychological, sexual or non-sexual: any kind of activity which involves a vigorous pelvic movement like running or dancing; the warmth of the sun or a hot bath, or floating in a calm sea; vibrations felt sitting on a bus or train; a word; a real or fantasized image; a touch, an idea, a kiss, that certain look in someone's eyes. You become aware that you feel turned on – perhaps specifically to one person, or more generally, with no particular person in mind.

At this point choice and circumstance will dictate what happens next. If it's the wrong time or place or you don't feel sufficiently in the mood for whatever reason, it may well go no further. But should you decide to pursue your felt desire your body will tend to follow a pattern of response as the level of arousal increases.

On the outside looking in

The traditional method of illustrating this pattern is by dividing the cycle into four stages: excitement, plateau, orgasm and resolution.

Excitement. The blood flow is increased which brings about changes in the nervous system, making certain parts of your skin more sensitive. Your nipples become erect, your clitoris becomes hard and erect. Your inner and outer lips engorge with blood making them puff up and change colour. The glands in your vagina issue a lubricating fluid.

Plateau. The nerve endings are even more highly sensitized through the build-up of blood, particularly in your pelvic area. Your vagina balloons out, especially if you are enjoying something going in and out of it. The p.c. muscle swells with blood, sometimes creating a desire for penetration or pressure against the outside of your vagina.

Orgasm. With continuous stimulation and an uncluttered nervous system, the tension, like air in a tyre, will seek release automatically Orgasm is a reflex response, like that of the sphincter muscle when released by pressure inside the rectum: a useful, if unromantic, analogy!

Resolution. With the release of tension, your heart rate, your blood pressure returns to normal. Your body readjusts and gradually your skin loses its extra sensitivity and the genital tissue returns to its normal state, although you may find your labia can still feel tender and puffy the morning after the night before.

On the inside looking out

Now look at this process more subjectively and see if this describes any of your own experience.

Gathering momentum. The gentle current begins to gather strength; you may feel wetness in your vagina, a genital stirring, a swirling in your abdomen. On one occasion you gather momentum quickly, at other times you may feel gently aroused for a long time. However long it takes, if you continue doing whatever it is that is arousing you, you near the edge.

Nearing the edge. This stage is experienced as being on the point of orgasm but not quite. Certain parts of your body are able to receive more and more stimulation. You may notice a lot of muscular tension, especially in your genitals which can create the desire for penetration or pressure on your vagina. As the ring of muscle swells, it reduces the opening to the vagina which often makes it feel tighter. Anything inside feels harder and bigger, but in reality it is your own body which causes the sensation.

The tension reaches a point where it needs to be released. As women get close to orgasm, they usually need an unbroken rhythm of stimulation to be able to go over the edge. So, if a partner changes a stroke or moves slightly, it can slow you down temporarily. If this happens, you may feel frustrated and blame the other person but if you understand what has happened, you can simply allow yourself to go with the current again. You soon get back to where you were.

Waterfall. With a steady rhythm, the water reaches the edge and falls. As the build-up of tension in your pelvis is released, you feel the contractions in your vagina. If you have contracted other muscles, you may feel those releasing as well. These contractions will feel strong or light depending on how aroused you are and how much tension has accumulated. They can last a few seconds or spread spasmodically over a few minutes. If you are very aroused, you may notice a series of contractions like a series of mini-waterfalls either building or decreasing in intensity – these are known as multi-orgasms. You may experience this release without feeling contractions at all, but as more of a 'peaking' sensation, or reaching of an internal point of satisfaction and fulfilment.

Subsidence. If the tension is released, everything in your body slows down. At this point, you may feel energized and ready to take on the world, ravenously hungry or utterly exhausted, ready to curl up contently and go to sleep.

Sometimes strenuous fucking, or any sexual activity which involves moving the pelvis vigorously, will have the same effect of dispersing the blood without the need for orgasm. On the other hand, if you have been very aroused and feel high and dry, and don't do anything about it, you can still feel tension and congestion.

Arousal versus distraction. During any physical activity we can become engrossed in enjoyment of our bodies: running, gardening, climbing, speeding on a motor bike, breastfeeding, painting or belly dancing! Whether the activity is strenuous, stretching, playful or tranquil, we can forget the outside for a while and become absorbed with what's happening inside our bodies. For those moments, we can enjoy the luxury of forgetting what we look like or who will think what: we lose self-consciousness and our minds and bodies can work in unison. The same applies to sex. As your body follows the cycle just described, you will correspondingly become less aware of your surroundings – the more engrossed you are, the less conscious you are. This means that in a high state of arousal you won't be distracted by the awful colour of the wallpaper; you won't feel cold; you can become less aware of pain and discomfort; headaches or fatigue will temporarily disappear.

The decrease in sensitivity to what is happening *outside* our bodies will be matched by an increase in sensitivity to what is going on *inside* our bodies. Extra nerve sensitivity both heightens our awareness and alters our perception of a smell or taste or touch or sound so that the erotic dimension is enhanced and the more we like a particular stimulus, the more our bodies will tell us how exciting and pleasurable it is. With the increasing strength of the sensations, we become absorbed in them to the exclusion of everything else. Images and sensations take the place of thought and, as the level rises, we tend to become more singularly focused on one image or one sensation: our minds and genitals interact as one. The intensity of the focus affects our physical systems, which increase the focus in our minds and so on, until at some point we can feel as if we 'leave' our bodies – we experience a peak of this excitement and reach a point of union which some describe as an experience of transcending.

As we come down physically, we experience coming down mentally as well. As soon as arousal drops, we become aware of our surroundings again. For example, whereas a few minutes before, you may have been blissfully unaware of stiffness or soreness, suddenly you realize your leg has gone to sleep or your vagina feels a little the worse for wear!

Sexual difficulties and lack of interest in sex can often be traced back to insufficient arousal. Although many women tend to depend on

partners for the achievement of sexual stimulation and satisfaction, the key to arousal lies not in our lovers but in *ourselves*: we need to ensure the optimum conditions for our own enjoyment and recognize the difference between being aroused and not.

There are purely physical factors which may make it difficult or impossible for us to get sexually excited: tiredness, recent surgical or medical treatment, hormonal levels, nausea, the effect of alcohol, pain or physical tenderness or discomfort, various kinds of medication including anti-depressants and tranquillizers, even being too cold or too hot. These factors tend to diminish desire for sexual activity at the outset so the process of arousal won't even get started. But sometimes, a sudden pain or sensation interrupts the flow and causes a decrease in enjoyment.

Anxiety. There are all kinds of passion-killers which adversely affect our enjoyment, but the biggest passion-killer of them all is anxiety. At a physiological level, anxiety will block the initial responses in the brain which start the arousal process, and at any stage during the cycle it will restrict the blood. This will alter our perception of sensations, which means we are more likely to be distracted than absorbed. And the more distracted we are, the less our bodies can respond. I have also noticed in myself and from discussions with other women that loss of arousal can lead to being an 'observer'. This describes the experience of looking at yourself and your partner from *outside* your body, watching everything in progress and going through the motions but feeling very detached and cut off from any direct physical enjoyment.

Anxiety stems from countless sources: fear of disapproval, that it's going to hurt, that you're taking too long, that you're not going to come, that you won't come up to scratch, that you'll look ugly, you might make a noise, the children might wake up, the neighbours might hear, you might get pregnant. You may be worried about all sorts of external problems with friends or at work, or what to cook tomorrow evening and will you hear the alarm in the morning?

Apart from practical worries there are less tangible factors which cause a lot of havoc. Have you ever had the experience of being absorbed in your body, melting into enjoyment, forgetting everything else when suddenly an image or thought darts through your mind and before you know what's happened, you are back in your head again? This is the mark of the personal prude (see opposite).

Personal prudes. These represent unconscious messages about sex from sexual stereotypes (see Chapter 3) or past sexual experiences. Rationally we can dismiss the message as absurd but it can still inhibit

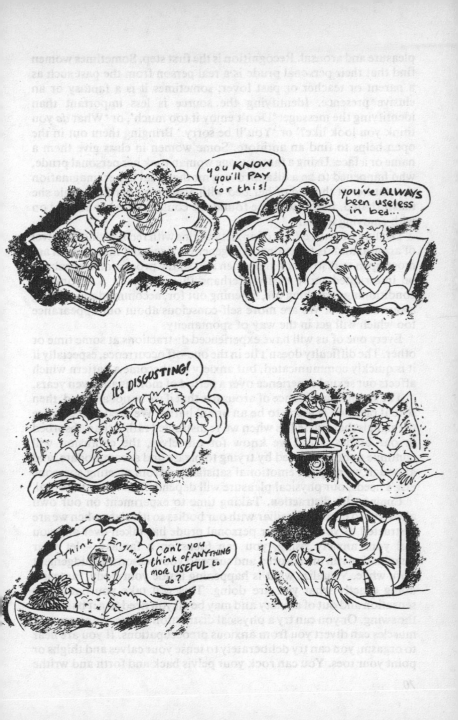

pleasure and arousal. Recognition is the first step. Sometimes women find that their personal prude is a real person from the past such as a parent or teacher or past lover; sometimes it is a fantasy or an elusive presence. Identifying the source is less important than identifying the message: 'Don't enjoy it too much', or 'What *do* you think you look like?' or 'You'll be sorry.' Bringing them out in the open helps to find an antidote. Some women in class give them a name or a face. Using a fantasy, one woman took her personal prude, who happened to be a disapproving mother, and in her imagination she put her at the end of her bed with a smile on her face while she masturbated. In this way she found she could ignore her and get on with enjoying herself.

Dealing with the effects of anxiety begins with recognizing our level of arousal and its functions. It is generally accepted that women are more open to distraction than men and so the process of arousal can be interrupted more easily. Perhaps this is due to a lifetime of conditioning: watching for, listening out for, accommodating, being aware of *others*. We are more self-conscious about our appearance too which will get in the way of spontaneity.

Every one of us will have experienced distractions at some time or other. The difficulty doesn't lie in the one-off occurrence, especially if it is quickly communicated, but anxiety can become a pattern which affects our sexual experience over a period of months and even years.

The simple significance of arousal is that if we're not aroused, then sexual pleasure is going to be an uphill battle. We need to recognize the signals that will tell us when we're distracted rather than absorbed in our bodies. Until we know for ourselves, the confusion will continue to be reinforced by trying to please and accommodate, and although we may get emotional satisfaction from meeting someone else's needs, our physical pleasure will depend on sufficient arousal.

Coping with distraction. Taking time to experiment on our own allows us to become familiar with our bodies so it's clear when we are distracted. If you find your personal prude has taken over and you feel your anxiety rising, you can focus on a fantasy – let your imagination run uncensored and suspend your reason and judgement for a while. Visualize what is happening inside your body, fantasize doing exactly what you are doing. This will take you back into sensation and out of anxiety and may be all you need to get back into the swing. Or you can try a physical distraction – squeezing your p.c. muscles can divert you from anxious preoccupations. If you are near to orgasm, you can try deliberately to tense your calves and thighs or point your toes. You can rock your pelvis back and forth and writhe around a bit! Breathing can also help you regain your focus. Follow your breathing, allow your jaw to drop, make an earthy sound. All of these can help you get out of your head and into your body again.

Avoid overkill. Remember, there is a fine line between staying with it and overkill. Learn the difference in your own body. It is essential not to persist in 'pleasuring' yourself or being stimulated by another person when it is more like a chore. If you try and get lost in pleasure but realize that you are just not in the mood, it is better to stop and choose a pleasurable diversion instead. If you are with a partner you can admit to being distracted instead of going against what your body is telling you. Tolerance of sexual activity risks dishonouring you, your body and your partner as well.

Finally, remember that if you don't know what's happening, you can't really expect anyone else to: it is your body after all. Because we tend not to experiment on our own, we tend not to understand when we're on the way up or the way down; we inhibit and over- or underestimate our own arousal.

If you are not familiar with your own pattern, you can easily assume that you are more aroused than you are. So can your partner. Because women don't have a visible erection, the feel of a wet vagina or the sight of an upstanding nipple can signal 'whoopee' to a partner who, in all good faith, believes that this heralds a state of sexual readiness that is in fact a long way off. These particular changes occur so early on in the cycle that a woman may need a lot more stimulation and time before she is ready emotionally and physically (if at all) for the big time! Such misunderstandings can cause problems but are easily avoidable with self-knowledge. Knowing and trusting your body makes a world of difference.

Following on

1. To experience for yourself a simple illustration of the difference between sensation and thinking, you could ask someone to massage your hand for five minutes. The massage doesn't need to be professional in any way – simply a variety of gentle and firm strokes, back and front, over the palm, the wrist, between the fingers, over the fingertips. Lie in a comfortable and restful position and give the other person the weight of your hand. As you receive, notice when thoughts intrude: e.g. 'How much time is left?', 'I'm not really comfortable', 'I wonder where he learned to do this?' 'Is she going to expect me to do the same for her?' Thoughts will take you *away* from your sensations.

Practise concentrating on each movement, being *in* your hand, feeling every stroke as it goes over your skin, feeling the effect on the rest of your body. Notice how you can go in and out of your head. One side-effect is the possibility of enjoying it so much that you will ask for the other hand to receive the same attention!

2. You may want to give in return. Again, notice when you are totally absorbed in what you are doing, focusing on this small part of someone's body, intent on pleasuring it. Notice, too, if you get distracted: 'Am I doing the right thing?', 'How much time has gone?', 'I wonder where I could do a course in massage?'

3. You might recognize a personal prude of your own. You could identify it with a name or a face and identify the message. It will usually be simple and short! Try and find a way to defuse it by creating a different image or phrase.

8

The Role of Fantasy

For most women and men, the phrase 'sexual fantasy' automatically conjures up an image of a film-set where they create their own production: a cast of thousands, or maybe just two, with some kind of script, often wordless, to follow from an initial sexual overture through to an orgasmic finale. This is, of course, what many people experience as sexual fantasy, but it is only one aspect of it. And since the concepts and taboos about human sexuality have for centuries been formed along the lines of male sexual experience, sexual fantasy has come to be defined almost exclusively in visual terms while the other senses have been ignored.

When we ask questions about sexual fantasies in a class, women will usually begin by asking themselves if they have 'film' experiences. The answer is very often no. Before looking at the fantasies which some women do experience, it's important to look first at how fantasy affects *all* of us in sexual situations, even if we're not aware of it.

Remember the parallel processes in arousal – the more you *feel* sensations in your body, the less you *think* in your head. When we're highly aroused, we suspend rational thought and judgement. We become less conscious of our surroundings – temporarily we leave behind the roles and responsibilities and expectations of our lives. As this happens, as our minds become merged with the sensations in our bodies, especially our genitals, an interplay develops: sensation blurs into fantasy and fantasy blurs into sensation. The more turned on you are, the more difficult it is to separate one from the other. The very sensations you become absorbed in give rise to images, colours, shapes, sounds. For example, focusing intently on your cunt can inspire a giant flower with a tiny golden core inside; your vagina ballooning out can become an enormous tunnel with waves crashing around; fingers moving in and out become a rod of gold, healing deep inside, touching the very heart of you; a penis becomes ten feet long, reaching deep within, filling you with molten gushes of liquid; you can be enveloped in a crimson shroud; see flowers, colours, jewels. Some people find that, instead of going inside their bodies, they go outside and, in fantasy, take off into the universe and stars.

It is a magical mechanism we have available to us if we are open to it: the more we are open to pleasure, the more we will find, which makes us more open, and so on. And the important thing to realize is that this mechanism is in our *own* bodies – it can be shared with another person, but it is part of ourselves.

Enjoyment of fantasy doesn't affect the reality. The penis is never ten feet long but sometimes the fantasy is so strong that we believe it actually happens. One woman who imagined her orgasmic contractions as powerful, huge movements, looked in the mirror when she masturbated one day, and was most disappointed to see not even a tiny little tremor! But it didn't alter her subjective experience. This phenomenon explains why even women who know the correct anatomical measurements of the vagina can still believe that their vaginas are really huge long tunnels waiting for penetration by a huge long penis. It also explains why many women who've just enjoyed the contractions of orgasm are bewildered and even indignant when their male partners ask them if they've come or not. How can they possibly have missed the earthquake!

The erotic components of fantasies prevalent in our culture reflect very closely the experience of female and male conditioning. The components of these fantasies are usually visual with emotional overtones. Remembering the whole cultural heritage of sex as a fearsome monster, as something which cannot be talked about or known about, it's hardly surprising that a frequent element in fantasies is whatever is *taboo*.

Taboo people, places and activities. We imagine sex with a forbidden person – a 'star', a neighbour, a stranger, someone else's partner, the woman next to you on the bus, the man in the estate agent's office, a child, maybe the pet Alsatian! The location can be a church, a supermarket, in the middle of the road, a train, your parents' bedroom, a beach, the dentist's chair – anywhere which is usually considered forbidden! What you actually do can be taboo as well: making love with a woman if you are heterosexual, enjoying group sex with dozens of partners all adoring you and ready to serve your every whim, sitting over your partner's face and being pleasured by an athletic tongue. It can be anything that you don't want or feel able to do in real life.

Watching and being watched. This is a direct effect of the secrecy of sex which we learn very early. The fantasy may involve spying through a keyhole or watching someone else in the same room as you. It includes sexual activity in public view, being blatantly exhibitionist, putting on a solo or joint performance in the middle of the park or on a stage.

Powerful and powerless. As sex has developed such a symbolism of power in our culture, we find this thread interwoven into many fantasies – sex becomes a commodity to be granted as a favour or withheld as a punishment. Women fantasize having this power with one or more men, who are rampant with desire but kept at arm's length. Sometimes this is expressed by wanting to penetrate a man with your own imaginary penis.

The cultural stereotypes of female sexuality also find their way into women's fantasies. Here are some examples:

Prostitute

I imagine I'm a prostitute, in high boots, with men queueing up to take me.

I'm in a seedy club, dark and smoky and picked up by a stranger.

I'm serving in a men's drinking club, with the shortest of short skirts and nothing on underneath. When men touch me I look surprised, though secretly enjoying it!

In fantasy we can enjoy the pleasure and power of availability without degradation.

Superlay

I just glide silently into action with a fellow traveller in the tiniest compartment, somehow we just fuck and climax and then go our separate ways without a word.

In fantasy we can enjoy sexual freedom and no fear of consequences.

Eve

I lie there masturbating gently, arousing the man who doesn't want to come because he will demean himself; somehow he'll lose points, but he cannot help himself and has a huge ejaculation!

In fantasy we can enjoy the power of being the one in control.

Virgin

I'm sitting in front of a class or being interviewed, wearing a long skirt and someone comes underneath me and begins to pleasure me under my skirt folds. I have to continue to teach and keep a straight innocent face while the waves of tension and pleasure get stronger and stronger. I get redder and redder, and wonder will they notice, and somehow I come.

In fantasy, we can enjoy being outrageous!

Madonna

I'm lying there with my legs spread wide apart on a huge velvet couch and, one by one, these tall muscular men with huge quivering erections are led up to me, and their penises guided into me. They are weeping with relief to enter me, and so aroused that they begin to come after only a few deep slow strokes – then they quicken and give their all, flowing into me and out of me. Then exhausted and grateful they bow down with respect, saluting the great queen, while I lie unmoving, hugely capacious, awaiting the next.

In fantasy, we can generously and lovingly accommodate the needs of others without loss of honour and status.

Perhaps you recognize some of these elements in your own fantasies. Other components stem from our own experience: we may relive past memories of sexual and enjoyable interludes or even just fragments of them which bring back the feelings of that time. Or sometimes we focus on the future: you may be on your way to see your lover and the train's late, so you imagine what you'll do when you set eyes on each other! Or you may imagine a whole encounter involving someone you know who, for some reason, is taboo.

In tune with the arousal process, some women may start by imagining a setting which is conducive to pleasure; a moonlit beach, a forest, snow, sunny fields, lying in warm water, a palm-fringed lagoon. With more arousal, the image can become more detailed. Like stopping a film on a single frame and repeating it over and over again, you may find your unconscious mind selects an erotic detail – the curve of the buttocks, the in movement of his penis, the expression on her face, or the sound of a groan or a sigh, or the sensation of someone's lips.

Some women find that their visual imagery takes on more abstract and less human form. Imagine, for example, lying on the carpet with your legs resting on the settee wide apart as the sun streams in through the window all over your body. As you masturbate, you might concentrate more and more totally on the sun as a single powerful beam, slowly entering you, lighting up every dark corner inside your body until your whole body is filled with sunlight and pleasure. You may like to incorporate other elements like water or air into your own fantasies. One woman I know has a particularly close relationship with trees!

To be able to fantasize in these ways is not a must – simply giving yourself one more goal or another reason to feel inadequate is counter-productive. Sometimes we are inhibited because of misunderstanding the nature of fantasy. These are some of the fears expressed in a group.

'If I describe my fantasy to anyone else, it will spoil the fantasy.' Women can fear that the telling will somehow take away the magic and the power. Although no one is ever forced to share a fantasy, we have found that it is possible to recount a fantasy in a class without losing its sexual potency. Of course, we need to feel safe to do so. First, because it means confronting our embarrassment of we do have sexual images, and our chagrin if we don't. Also we fear that someone else may laugh or be shocked. It's true that what turns on one person is often a mystery to another but, even so, fantasies, however wide-ranging and varied, can be enjoyed together. Another difficulty which arises is due to the pressure to be all things to all people: many women are offended and hurt if their partner reveals a fantasy as it makes them feel inadequate. If you've never fantasized yourself, you're more likely to feel insulted. Sometimes it happens the other way round. Sharing a fantasy with a partner can cause misunderstanding but many women have enjoyed doing so with their partners, and have sometimes created joint fantasies which can be enjoyed together.

'If I fantasize, there's a risk I might do it in real life.' As a person we make many choices and decisions; we have moral and ethical and ideological values. Remember that a fantasized situation works only because most of that other self is suspended for a while. Fantasy provides a mental playground where we can explore and maybe enjoy the forbidden elements in ourselves with impunity.

For example, imagine masturbating on the dining table in a boardroom, arousing the up-tight business executives around the table as they try to ignore what's happening and eat their soup. Fantasy is one thing, but imagine the reality. Just the thought of the crumbs on the cloth is off-putting!

You may have a fantasy which you would like to try out for real as opposed to those which you would never dream of bringing into the light of day. But even if you do enact a fantasy for real, it will be a different experience because you will have to relate to the *total* situation, not just *part* of it.

A fantasy, for example, about being with two partners at once can be erotically stimulating precisely because it eliminates personal and social considerations: other people's feelings of exclusion, jealousy or competition, your own anxiety about coming up to scratch, concern about who sleeps where, what to provide for breakfast in the morning and *what* are you all going to talk about! Sex with a complete stranger on a train works in fantasy because you don't run the risk of VD or pregnancy and because, in fantasy, your tights aren't an embarrassing barrier to the spontaneous and wordless flow of it all. All those elements which fantasy eliminates will be included in reality.

'*If I fantasize when we're making love, it's disloyal.*' This stems from the cultural dictum that sex should be spontaneous and natural. I believe in cultivating a healthy mistrust of anyone who tells you that anything you might be doing or feeling sexually indicates that you are falling short in some way. Sexuality is an area in which we are *all* vulnerable – it's just that some people hide their sexual vulnerability by claiming to be expert in the sexual behaviour of others.

Since, particularly as women, we have become so detached from our bodies and are so open to distraction and self-consciousness, it can be extremely useful to use a fantasy – either a visual image or just a deliberate sinking into bodily sensations – when we're aware of losing or have lost our erotic impetus. As soon as we become conscious that we are thinking about the time we're taking or worried about something, we can help ourselves back into pleasure. It is a wonderful short-term help, especially if we know that we are prone to anxiety in certain situations. Each women can learn about her personal use for fantasy in a way that is helpful to her enjoyment of sexual activity.

Fantasy is a way of helping deal with the truth of the situation for many women. We know that realistically we may not be able to avoid anxiety and distraction. Knowing how to help yourself prevents blaming a partner and can also short circuit a total drop in sexual arousal. When self-consciousness interrupts enjoyment, some women imagine a picture of what is happening and incorporate the *real* person into a fantasy. The extra dimension provided by the fantasy enhances sensations and dispels the rising anxiety.

It can also be helpful to know your personal prudes and use

fantasy to countermand them. One of my fantasies takes place on the top of a Mexican pyramid. While I am being pleasured by at least three people, a crowd is all around, at a slight distance, cheering, singing in celebration, applauding me on! Although the fantasy will have to remain in my head, one of the key elements for me is the absolute permission for pleasure, which counteracts the gloomy cautions of my personal prude.

On the other hand, it can be unwise to use fantasy to avoid the truth: if fantasy is the *only* way you can tolerate the person or activity then it could be kinder to yourself and your partner to confront the situation more openly and directly.

This brings us to the inevitable darker side of fantasy – violence in ourselves and in men. Women worry about the elements in their fantasies which are sadistic or masochistic. In one way fantasy, like any other kind of daydream, can act as a safety-valve for strong but inappropriate feelings. We may use ordinary fantasies to seek revenge and express murderous intent in non-sexual situations, and sexual fantasy too can allow us to turn the tables, to reverse the roles of power. But this may set up a personal conflict.

'*How can I be an assertive and capable, strong woman and yet enjoy fantasies of submission or rape?*' The process of self-development means gradually breaking away from norms and received models, but those models are *always* there. We simply develop alternative ways of behaving. However assertive we can be at times, there will always be a submissive and an aggressive part of us, which present a constant daily choice of behaviour and response. Similarly, we know that the various sexual models are part of us, part of our heritage as women, not only from our parents but way beyond that. Fantasy can be a way of acknowledging the presence of these stereotypes without feeling bad or guilty but simply accepting them.

A fantasy of rape is totally different from the reality. In fantasy, a woman, as fantasizer, has *total control* over what happens. In reality she has none. In fantasy, she can be aroused and feel pleasure through her body because she eliminates unwanted stimuli which would interfere: in reality her body cannot begin to be aroused because fear will close down all the systems involved in arousal. In reality, blood actually leaves the genitals so her body is in a state where no physical pleasure can possibly be experienced. Her vagina can be opened and forced entry can take place but as it is tight and unaroused her experience will be one of extreme pain which results in extensive soreness, internal bruising and lacerated tissue. And yet, in the face of this quite elementary information, we *still* choose to believe that women actually enjoy the reality of rape.

Violence, fantasy and pornography

Until a couple of years ago, I took a professionally permissive attitude to pornography, along the lines that after so much taboo, an attitude of permission rather than repression was more beneficial. However, after reading some of the excellent research and literature from a woman's point of view, I could no longer feel comfortable.

It presents a series of dilemmas. I believe it is important for women to look at pornographic material because seeing and acknowledging can be more empowering than hiding away from something. It is also important that women should not be made to feel disloyal to other women if they find conventional pornography arousing: we have not been brought up in a culture which offers a positive female sexual image as an alternative.

The damage that is done so blatantly in a pornographic context when a man is shown violently abusing a woman or when her genitals are displayed in humiliation, is more insidiously achieved on a day-to-day basis. In ordinary advertisements, media images affect a far greater number of people far more often with far more subtlety. Against this we have no protection at all.

What is important is for us to talk to each other about our own experience and to clarify our feelings and attitudes. Fantasy can be useful as a plaything but is not recommended as a crutch. It can help us to block out interfering messages or distracting thoughts. It is a useful adjunct to sexual exploration. It is also one way to develop an erotic imagination and a *personal* definition of what is sexually appealing. The next step is for us, as women, to create our own erotic images, make our own erotic forms, spin our own erotic yarns.

In Chapter 7 we looked at the physiological reality of orgasm: the muscular release of tension caused by congestion. Although it is only one relatively short part of sexual experience, orgasm holds a particular fascination. Some people believe that the release generates electrical energy. Others have advocated abstention from orgasm (particularly for men) as a way of conserving valuable energy which can be converted to a more spiritual plane. The history of orgasm, and its relevance to women's sexuality in a western culture, has resulted in a series of emotional and physical pressures which have given women even more grounds for feeling self-conscious and sexually inadequate.

Many women today will be able to recognize changes in attitudes to orgasm within the course of their own lives. First of all for women, in common with other female animals, orgasm was considered irrelevant – the female human doesn't need an orgasm for reproduction, therefore it was unimportant. This view still prevails in certain cultures today, even in our own where notable gurus insist that the trend of the last decade which encourages women to strive for orgasm consciously is harmful because it risks raising unrealistic and unnecessary expectations.

The first significant change was the division of orgasms into clitoral and vaginal, immature and mature respectively. The vaginal orgasm became the first goal for the Sexually Mature and Fulfilled Woman. But she couldn't rest long on her laurels because a second trend appeared – towards simultaneous orgasm – which required meticulous attention to timing and perfect attunement with her partner.

This took some working at but, eventually, BINGO! Unfortunately, not long after, researchers discovered that women could experience *multiple* orgasms so, for the Sexually Mature and Fulfilled Woman, one was simply not enough! Then came the proclamation of the 'G' spot (G for Grafenberg), a special area of the anterior vaginal wall which was suddenly launched into stardom as a trigger for orgasms and a process called female ejaculation. Women sometimes experience discharge on orgasm and it was previously thought that this was either urine (in all the excitement) or unusually copious vaginal discharge. But when the fluid was examined under the microscope it was discovered to be neither – instead the substance was found to be identical to the prostate fluid which is produced by a gland in men's bodies and mixed with the semen. No one is yet sure where it comes from in women.

And next? In America, there are already popular weekend workshops entitled, 'Extended Sexual Orgasms – How to Achieve', attended by husbands who accompany their wives in the hope that they will reach even more Sexual Maturity and Fulfilment by learning how to prolong the actual physical experience of orgasmic contractions. Better start timing now!

Because this relatively small part of our whole sexual experience has been given undue emphasis in the past, I was tempted to omit it altogether from this book in an attempt to redress the balance. But, on the other hand, it is difficult for women to avoid concerns about orgasm, whether having one is actually a problem for them or not.

For nine years orgasm felt like a millstone round my neck. I wasn't having them and although I didn't quite know what it was I wasn't having, I felt terribly inadequate. It was something I would never dare to admit to and, even when I eventually discovered my clitoris and orgasm, it still continued as an obsession. I would still wonder whether or not I would come because I was sure this was a key part of my sexual viability. Sometimes, I wish that I'd never heard of the word as it can still so easily emerge as a psychological pressure and goal which ruins spontaneous enjoyment.

Some of this will be familiar to others as well. Although many women have never experienced any difficulty in reaching orgasm, the vast and detailed media coverage has ensured that whether a woman is in a sexual relationship with a man or another woman, it is difficult to avoid the implicit assumption that orgasm is an *essential* part of a sexual interaction. We have been so profoundly affected that orgasm is seen as an imperative for one or both partners and we believe any sexual experience is incomplete without an orgasm somewhere to mark the finishing point. It has become a fixed point of reference, without which most of us wouldn't know where we were going or how to tell when we'd got there!

As it has become such a common point of reference, I decided to include orgasm despite my reluctance to endorse its importance any further. It will take a huge shift of awareness to put orgasm back into perspective but it can help in the meantime to look at some common misunderstandings and problems. As we've seen from the last chapter, confusion and anxiety interfere with our physical enjoyment and arousal. Worry about taking too long stems from one such misconception which, along with most things in this culture, promotes the idea that fastest is best. It's really quite ludicrous that consideration of time should even enter into the question of sexual enjoyment, but many of us have become vulnerable to this kind of performance pressure.

The *average* often quoted for a woman to reach orgasm from the beginning of the arousal process (i.e. from cold) is forty-five minutes. This is usually longer than women expect so the relief can be profound, unless of course you take forty-six minutes and then you can give yourself a really hard time!

Even more of a problem for many women is the quality of the actual experience when they finally achieve it. Because of the extra importance attributed to orgasm, the quality of this part of a woman's sexual experience has been assumed by men, and therefore women, to be an indication of her emotional and 'womanly' capacities. In order to clarify some of the confusion between different kinds of orgasm, it is helpful to separate the physical and the emotional factors.

Physical factors. On a purely physiological level, we know that every orgasm is the same: the tension and congestion in the pelvis caused by the stimulation of a vast network of nerves is released in orgasm, whether a woman reaches orgasm by stimulation of her nipples alone, by squeezing her thighs together, penetration of her vagina or direct contact with her clitoris. Objectively the orgasm is the same. But, of course, it can *feel* different. One of the reasons sensations vary in intensity is the changing level of excitement and the level of arousal. Another is the energy level, including general health and hormone balance.

In Chapter 7, we saw how the process of arousal affects our perception of our sensations, and this is why we feel the experience of orgasm in different places and in different ways. Sometimes the effect may spread through our bodies, sometimes it feels more specifically located in the vagina or in the clitoris because, whatever is happening in our bodies in general, we will be more focused on a specific point.

Women describe 'clitoral' orgasm as 'more on the surface', 'more outside', 'more intense', 'more concentrated', 'more powerful', whereas 'vaginal' orgasms are described as 'inside', 'deeper', 'less specific', 'gentle contractions', 'a feeling of peaking', 'more diffuse'. Since the clitoris has so many nerve endings and the inner two-thirds of the vagina none, it is understandable that if an orgasm is felt around the clitoris it will feel more 'intense' and inside the vagina as more 'diffuse'.

Emotional factors. If you are reading this section hoping to pick up a few more clues as to how to achieve vaginal orgasms, you will have fallen into the trap of considering vaginal orgasms, not as different from clitoral orgasms, but as *superior*. Although physiological fact show us that every orgasm involves both the clitoris and the vagina, it is the emotional factors of investment and symbolism which dominate our imagination. Some women express a greater emotional satisfaction with a vaginal orgasm because of the physical and emotional reality of being filled, of being complete. This is enhanced by a psychological and social dependence on that other person for personal and sexual significance which is conferred from the outside.

The physical stimulus is easily confused with this emotional need. Consequently, the enjoyment of a vaginal orgasm can have less to do with sensation than with the perception of fulfilment. This is why many women still look to vaginal orgasm as *the* goal.

To understand vaginal orgasm more realistically, we need to return to the physical realm. While clitoral stimulation is fairly visible, it isn't easy to see what happens with stimulation of the vagina. Vaginal orgasm has long been associated with the idea that orgasm was achieved through penile thrusting alone, and that the woman's vagina was receptive to her partner's penis while her clitoris loitered redundantly on the sidelines. In fact, as the penis moves in and out, the motion pulls on the outer lips which in turn pull on the clitoral hood so the clitoris is still being stimulated, just indirectly. A woman's genitals are still active. Her ability to feel an orgasm in her vagina is affected by the relative position of her clitoris and vagina and also by her arousal. Some women say that they have experienced this kind of orgasm when they felt very horny and very much wanting penetration so this heightened arousal will have focused and increased the tension of the p.c. muscle.

It is important to understand that the physical experience of a certain sensation and the emotional experience are *separate* although they can be enjoyed together. For example, vaginal orgasm can be experienced through fingers penetrating the vagina so the sensation can be enjoyed without a penis at all. Similarly, the sensation of something in her vagina may make an orgasm much more *pleasurable* for a woman – this is not the same as believing she is dependent on a penis or, by definition, dependent on a male partner.

Sharing our experience and increasing our understanding can clarify some of these issues, but it is difficult to avoid colluding with the excessive concern shown about the mechanics. In an ideal situation, we wouldn't have to *learn* how to enjoy ourselves, but because we have become alienated from our bodies in so many ways, we have to relearn to experience what happens naturally!

While we are so busy concentrating on time or quality or location or length of orgasm, we can lose sight of the significance of the whole cycle of sexual excitement. Although we may conclude something is wrong because we didn't have an orgasm, the source of the difficulty will be found elsewhere. Often it lies in the element of trust. The mechanics have obscured this important aspect: trust in yourself and trust in another person.

Trust. The reason for trust is that for a short while we need to let go. Part of the fascination with the moment of orgasm is that we often experience a temporary out-of-the-body feeling, a temporary loss of rational control. This applies not only to the moment of orgasm but also to the experience of being very highly excited and aroused because, as we have seen, that very process requires us to become less present, less aware, less conscious. We need to be open and unafraid for this process to take effect.

Letting go of the controlled part of ourselves can evoke anxiety. Inhibitions stem from our personal prudes who warn us of looking silly or ugly or grotesque; they warn us of the danger of letting loose the animal, the Nymphomaniac. We might do something indecorous like grunt or groan or kick or bite – something uncontrolled which doesn't fit a feminine or maternal or attractive image. Some women report that their partners have indicated a certain repugnance for 'over the top' behaviour, but often we carry those fears within ourselves.

One of the values of masturbation is to identify and confront these particular prudes, when we realize that we are afraid to let go. If we are familiar with our responses, we can trust our bodies that much more: if we value our bodies we will ensure that we are vulnerable only when we know we are genuinely safe.

If you had to leave something precious in someone else's temporary care, you would probably be extremely careful who that person was. You would need to trust that person implicitly to keep watch in your absence. In orgasm, we temporarily 'leave' our bodies and we let go control but since most of us don't care about or really inhabit our bodies, we dismiss the need for trust. Even though we ignore the wisdom of our bodies, they continue to protect us. Numbness, a feeling of distance and a lack of arousal affect our ability to let go in orgasm.

Probably because of a strong vaginal reflex, some women find it easier than others to be able to 'function' in adverse circumstances. The orgasm reflex can be triggered purely physiologically, in the same way that an orgasm can be produced by a vibrator applied to the clitoris. So by tensing the vaginal muscle, a physical release will occur and orgasm will be experienced locally and specifically without the need to be emotionally open and vulnerable.

More often than not, difficulty arises not from lack of physical safety but emotional safety. If we cannot express intense intimate feelings of anger or grief with a partner, we may find it difficult to express the vulnerability of sexual arousal. The relevance of emotional intimacy is often ignored although it affects our behaviour. Some women and men find it easier to let go sexually when they are with a stranger than with someone they are close to, and can find it easier to let their hair down with a part-time lover than a full-time partner.

If you know that you feel safe with your partner, you can still find difficulty sometimes in letting go because of your inability or your partner's inability to express important feelings with each other. Lack of emotional safety may also have little to do with the actual partner but with your own past fears and frustrations. Whatever the source, the important thing is to honour your responses rather than try to achieve some goal or do what you feel is expected. Trying to reach an orgasm in the face of feeling frantic, angry, resentful, desperate or numb, only entrenches those feelings even further. Learning to let go of the goal of orgasm is essential to our enjoyment of our bodies when masturbating or making love with a partner.

Remember that every controversy, every norm, every debate about orgasm emanated originally from the assumptions of experts observing and judging from the *outside* – no question or difficulty has ever spontaneously arisen from a woman's own experience! When a woman expresses difficulty in reaching orgasm it is a result of comparing herself to one of those norms.

Many of us find it difficult to trust and enjoy this intensely physical experience in our own unique way because it has become standardized, labelled and just another part of the outside reflection against which we rate and assess ourselves. Not even during these profound and private moments are we free from the need for outside approval!

If more time in the past had been devoted to looking at the optimum conditions for arousal, which takes up a relatively large part of any sexual interaction, instead of focusing exclusively on fifteen or so seconds that represent the finale, maybe we'd all be more relaxed and spontaneous. But what we can do now is renounce the tyranny of orgasm and reclaim the experience as one very personal and optional part of our sexual enjoyment.

10
Feelings

Few people understand the significance of their feelings. Although women tend to regard men as cut off from their feelings, both women and men fall into the trap of fragmentation again: the head is split from the heart, the mind from the body. What is felt in the genitals is assumed to be unconnected to what is happening in the rest of the body. This stems from a mistaken assumption about the nature of feelings and fear of emotions – that they suddenly descend from outside and take us over – rather than from an understanding that emotions produce physiological changes inside our bodies which prepare the body for appropriate action.

Most people have so lost touch with this process that they may never learn from the signals in their own bodies. They don't register that they feel sad or fearful or angry or hurt, so they don't identify or express those feelings. Unfortunately, contrary to popular opinion, feelings don't simply disappear. Whatever their source – whether it is the effect of one situation like the death of someone close to you or the regular experience of being criticized or ignored – they will continue to push for expression. Sometimes they emerge in our relationships so we find ourselves overreacting to someone or feeling inappropriately anxious or hostile or clinging, or we may feel overwhelmingly tired or depressed. Emotions connected with events long ago in childhood can undermine adult relationships, not because the emotions exist but because people refuse to *acknowledge* their existence. Unexpressed feelings can also play havoc with our bodies, adversely affecting the body's natural processes such as digestion, elimination of toxins, blood pressure, breathing and including, of course, sexual response.

There are three levels of expression of feelings. First, an acknowledgement to yourself, identifying what your body is telling you and taking some appropriate action to defuse or confront the situation. Second, verbal expression, a simple statement of how and what you feel. This allows you to handle your emotions and communicate more effectively and clearly with someone else. The third level is physical release of feelings, through tears or shouting or trembling. This is a capacity which we had as children. We were all able (for a while anyway) to express our feelings quite spontaneously without shame or embarrassment. Growing up entails learning control, which is necessary in some situations. But as far as emotions are concerned, we have learned to over-control, so we become less and less aware of them. Relearning to release our feelings physically takes time, but it can be done. It means learning how to recognize and open our bodies to the natural processes of release rather than closing up. This should be done in an appropriate and safe setting and some information is given at the end of the book for readers who feel they would like to explore this area further.

In a sexuality class, the expression of feelings is very relevant to our understanding of sexual experience. Physical expression is relevant to sexual response because sexual arousal in itself, as we have seen, involves a loss of control. Sometimes we hold back from sexual excitement and arousal because we do not want to lose control. Simply being in an aroused state physically means that we are more open and, as our control comes down, many feelings and tensions quite unrelated to sex can be discharged through the same channels as the physical tension of sexual arousal. This is why you might feel overwhelmed or burst into tears, or feel desperate or angry and want to hit out; you may experience shaking and trembling, sometimes after orgasm, sometimes before.

It's difficult to know where these feelings come from when there doesn't appear to be an obvious connection with the situation you're in or the person you're with. Many people feel deeply relaxed and released from a lot of psychological tension after sexual activity but *some* feelings cannot be released through orgasm alone. Orgasm is a *physical* release and, even though some tension and stress can be released, it won't help release deeper feelings – it will just provide a temporary improvement until the tension builds up again.

When we're aroused and more open, touching our bodies or being touched can evoke past memories. Sensations in and around our genitals arouse past sensations and associations – if these are positive and pleasurable they can increase our current pleasure, but if they are not, they will often get in the way. Feeling open and vulnerable and loved can stir up feelings of being open and hurt and ignored or betrayed. It's a very complex mechanism and there's no rational sequence or order, which is why it's so important to learn individually about ourselves.

It is valuable to make links between past experiences and emotions which we may have denied or buried in the hope that if we don't think about them, they will cease to be important! Time and time again, I find that we retain feelings, particularly associated with our bodies and genitals, that we are surprised to discover. Like everyone else in our culture, we believe that if we say goodbye to someone or something in our heads, it is the end of it. But our bodies always remember.

Sadness and grief. This can be grief at the loss of someone important, separation from someone you love or moving away from a place or people you have loved. But sometimes the grief can be more specific to physical experience – the loss of a child, a stillborn child, an abortion, a miscarriage. Sometimes our genitals won't respond, sometimes a numbness can spread to the rest of the body as well. Even though women think they have said goodbye to someone they have lost, there is a physical need to let those feelings out. After an abortion, one woman found she couldn't get interested in sex. She had talked about it with her partner and *thought* it was resolved but, like most of us, she hadn't given her body any room for feeling.

It is easy to underestimate the sadness at the loss of part of your body like a breast or your womb or regret at a loss of youth or a chance to conceive. One woman spoke of a relationship which had ended many years before and found that she had not been able truly to let go of the man involved. Another woman found that the death of her mother had affected her more profoundly than she had realized. You may feel sorrow at not knowing your body more intimately and sad at not having taken more care of it!

Anxiety and fear. Anxiety may be related to situations which are not connected directly to sexuality, but it can still have an effect: fear of losing a job, coping with a crisis, anticipating a confrontation or interview or a particular challenge on the horizon. We have looked in detail at the various sources of anxiety and how they interfere with sexual experience. We can suffer from anxiety about losing control, making the wrong impression, being interrupted and, sometimes, that anxiety becomes a deep fear – fear of being mistreated or abused or rejected. Past fears can also interfere. Traumatic abuse in childhood can continue to affect women's experience as adults. Such an experience will have varied effects – it may be acute shame about one's body, or revulsion towards sexual contact, a general numbness or holding back from intense enjoyment. And no amount of mechanical practice or psychological 'adjustment' will release the fear or anger.

Frustration and anger. In *A Woman in Your Own Right* I described two different levels of anger: there is a deep layer of anger ('root anger') which contains a powerful source of energy, and a top layer which relates more to past and present hurts and frustrations. If we look at the deeper layer first, we find a direct link between root anger and sexuality. Women often hold back from anger through fear of overwhelming, fear of being destructive, fear of losing control – the same fears we have when expressing our sexual feelings. Many women find it difficult to let go in anger and find it difficult to let go in orgasm. One of the links is physical. When we do express anger we feel very powerful and unstoppable, as we do when we feel a lot of sexual energy. We can feel attuned to our bodies in both contexts: we feel energy and strength and power in ourselves. One of the hormones released when we become aroused with anger is androgen – and androgen is known also to relate to sexual arousal, which is why it is administered experimentally to women in menopause as a corrective measure for loss of sexual desire. The very hormone that contributes to sexual desire (present in the male) is released when we express the emotion of anger. It is interesting to note that in most cultures *both* areas of women's behaviour are suppressed.

This positive kind of anger provides an impetus to learn and to move and to change – to make choices. All these are very relevant to sexual experiences when you can begin to assert yourself by knowing your body, by identifying what you want and by asking for it, by realizing that you have a right to be equal sexually as in every other way.

Because we spend so much of our time out of touch with this positive root anger, we tend to concentrate on expressing the top layer of resentment and frustration, and even that we sometimes find difficult to do directly. The expression tends to be indirect, and sexual relationships offer an ideal context. Early in our lives we learned that we had something that 'they' wanted so one obvious way of punishing someone, of indirectly communicating resentment and anger, is by withdrawing from sexual contact or refusing sexual intercourse.

Aggressive expression of anger is another option. The actual motion of penetration can become aggressive. In the use of words such as 'lay', 'bang', 'nail', 'give her one', and 'screw', male aggression and fucking become dangerously interwoven. But a woman too can use penetration aggressively, often finding in the friction and the pressure against her cervix, some temporary physical relief from her own deeper frustrations. Because of the similarity between sensations of anger and sexual arousal, some people find that sex after a fight is much 'better' and even pick a row beforehand knowing this. But it is important to distinguish between assertive anger which is expressing yourself as an equal and aggressive anger which easily tips over into lack of concern or consideration for the other person; it ceases to be an equal interaction when it degenerates into abuse or exploitation.

If we express anger passively we usually turn it inwards so the result is often depression, tiredness and illness – all of which will have a marked effect on our sexual behaviour.

Often psychological tension is echoed by tension in our genitals. One extreme example is vaginismus: the p.c. muscle goes into spasm, closing the vaginal entrance. This means that a woman cannot have intercourse even if she says she wants it because it is physically impossible. Her vagina is giving a very clear message of 'no'. One woman suffered from vaginismus very soon after her marriage. She discovered that the physical symptom was connected to her anger at feeling betrayed. Her marriage had been arranged and her husband-to-be had agreed that she could continue to wear western clothes and to study at university. However, as soon as the wedding had taken place, he and his family had exerted constant pressure on her to wear traditional clothing and to assume the conventional role of a wife at home. She could not express her anger verbally so her body expressed it for her.

Any one event can affect us with a whole combination of emotions. Diana had been told by her GP that she was 'frigid'. Six months before, her small son had been knocked down in a car accident. He had recovered but the whole episode had obviously been traumatic – her shock at the time, her worry about her child and her resentment towards her husband who she felt hadn't really supported her at this time of crisis as much as she had wanted. However, all three of them had survived the crisis and, as far as they were aware, it was just a very unpleasant memory. But Diana gradually found herself unable to respond to sexual overtures from her husband, less interested in intimacy, and soon not feeling anything at all when the normally sensitive parts of her body were touched. She drew further and further away until she went to her doctor for help. The intense feelings of shock and fear about her son and her harboured resentment towards her husband had never before been expressed. Once she'd realized this, she was able to let out some of the tears and tension she had been storing and was able to go back and talk through her feelings with her husband openly.

Physical trauma and pain. Apart from emotional scars, there are of course the visible scars. Again we make the mistake of assuming that once a wound has healed, that is the end of it. We forget that we are more than skin and tissue and that true healing requires more than medication. Our bodies can be abused, both legitimately and criminally and, in either situation, we tend to deny the pain. It is not easy to be honest about pain when cultural attitudes make it so difficult: we are encouraged to follow the stiff-upper-lip routine and not to cry out in labour because of upsetting other patients. It is a popular belief among lay and professional people alike that an inevitable consequence of being a woman and having a woman's body is to suffer. At a conscious level it is to be expected; more unconsciously, it is felt to be deserved. Western medicine further distances us from our bodies by anaesthetizing the whole process of recovery so that the process of healing becomes artificial.

Low self-esteem encourages us to become masochistic in relation to our bodies. Have you ever not cried out in pain because of what others might think? Have you ever found it difficult to express the extent of pain of menstruation to a doctor because you half believed that you have to suffer as a woman? Have you suffered the painful after-effects of episiotomy in silence because you felt too helpless to say anything? Have you ever put up with painful intercourse or discomfort during sexual activity without doing anything about it? Have you ever had an internal examination which felt too rough and not said anything? If you can answer yes to any of these, it is likely that you have stored a lot of pain in your body as well as the emotions of fear or rage.

We have learned to deny the pain we feel. We have learned to think of a breast or uterus removed as a missing part. Like an arm off a china doll, a missing breast is disfiguring and we are certain to register the effect on our appearance for we are still aware, after all, of the need to be decorative. A missing uterus may mean no more conception – we are still aware of our maternal function. But often we fail to grieve that missing part as part of the *whole*.

Exploring the links between unexpressed feelings and sexual response will show very clearly how, as women, we cannot be split off into separate little parts. Our actual experience is an interplay between our physical, emotional, intellectual and sexual selves. For this reason, we can sometimes find ourselves initiating or agreeing to a sexual encounter or perhaps deciding to masturbate and then finding that the real need lies *elsewhere* – this is why understanding our bodies is so important. You may find that you need a good cry or a cuddle or to be stroked or to punch a cushion and have a good yell or scream or take time to meditate or relax in some way – all of these physical needs are equally valid. It is important to see what you need and then meet that need, rather than rush to satisfy a genital itch when the need is not really for sex. We need to honour our bodies by recognizing what they are trying to tell us instead of consistently denying the knowledge that comes from a deeper and much wiser part of our being.

Loving your body is . . .

playing
saying it hurts when it does
saying no when you want to
having fun
enjoying closeness with another person
crying when you want to
attending to your gut reactions
jumping for joy occasionally
objecting to an offensive picture
asking for a foot massage
asking someone to move their fingers up and down just *there*
reading about your body
watching what you put inside it
stretching it fully
assertively moving away from a conversation when women are
    being ridiculed
breathing deeply
putting your feet up and asking for a cup of tea
becoming familiar with your hormonal changes
singing
looking in the mirror with pride
exercising for pleasure
laughing
resting
resting
resting!

Following on

1. You may like to do an exercise called 'Sexual Skeletons'. It identifies specific negative sexual and emotional experiences which may affect your present attitudes to yourself and in sexual relationships. Write down any events that come to mind. After each situation, write down who was involved. What did you experience emotionally? Did you experience any physical pain or discomfort? What did you really want to say or do at the time? How would you like to have handled that situation differently? You may then like to talk this through with someone else.

2. Another way to identify some of the past associations you have is to take thirty minutes with another person you trust and do the following: imagine you are speaking for your cunt, using 'I', and tell your story. It doesn't matter where you start. Be flexible and start with whatever comes to mind. It is fascinating to see what emerges and can help you recognize your feelings and connections with your past experience.

3. You can try some physical exercises to release tension.

a) Stand upright. Inhale deeply and then let yourself fall forward limply like a rag doll, with a loud full out-breath.

b) Lie on your back on the floor. Focus on your pelvis and rock it up and down. Slowly match your breath in and out to the movement: as you press downwards with your pubic bone, breathe in and as you press upwards, breathe out. After a few times, allow your jaw to relax and let yourself make a low sound as you breathe out. Don't go too fast, just practise a few times until you feel you want to stop.

c) For something more vigorous, lie on the floor, preferably on a carpet. As you lie there, bounce up and down on your buttocks, gently at first and then more energetically, remembering all the time to keep your jaw relaxed and to let a sound come out, starting softly but getting louder. Even if you end up laughing, it is a good way to relieve general tensions.

11

Once Upon a Time . . .

Sexual likes and dislikes can be difficult to identify with so many 'shoulds' and 'oughts' in our culture. A very illuminating exercise that we do in class is to compile an erotic guide – a list of as many 'turn-ons' and 'turn-offs' as you can think of. It is fun to let go a little and explore all your senses to find a range of tastes, smells, sounds, sensations and images. The illustration gives some idea of the sort of things you might find, but remember your list will be unique. When we share them in class we do find some in common, but often the very same item – for example, a tongue delving into your ear – can be for one woman a toe-curling delight, but for another an unspeakable irritation!

It is a useful way to draw together some of the learning so far and to see what conditions you find most congenial to sexual enjoyment. In this way you can actually take practical steps towards avoiding things you don't like and encouraging those you do. For example, you may find that time is important to you or the element of anticipation, in which case a quick grab is unlikely to turn you on very much. You may find psychological pressure disabling. You may get a kick out of someone else obviously relishing whatever they are absorbed in doing to you, whereas if you suspect they are only going through the motions on your behalf you may feel inhibited. You may be bored by predictability or reassured by it. Only you will know. You can find some conditions that are always important for you – for example, no chance of interruption – and you may find elements change depending on your mood or the person you're with. The important

TURN ONS

Surprise	Fresh bed linen
rain on car roofs	Old 60s singles
Smell of garlic FRYING	Peaches / olives
Alto Sax	earthy sounds
firelight	Being abroad!
wearing no knickers	forbidden places
Swimming naked	Dancing
Lychees.	Someone else's enjoyment of having me...
bikini marks	
buttons being undone slowly...	Unexpected touches
	Lying on beaches
Names...	Subtlety.
rolling in hay!	No clothes.
power of pleasing someone else	Them not!

TURN OFFS

Pressure of —	bedtime feelings
time, performance orgasm; bladder	untinished
cold	Lack of closeness
worry	being mocked
telephone	bad breath
alcohol	smell of mens SWEAT
grubby sheets	tongue in my ear.
crusty	Someone's expressed DISTASTE for ANY part of my body.
tired	
Painful	Predictability
	Anything when I'm not aroused.

Turn Ons

Certain body smells. / Strawberries in unusual places.
My back being held
Rain on roof at night. Sun on back.
Coconut sun oil. / Some men's bums.
Champagne m
Kissing, when aroused / Autumn evenings.
Some fantasies
Choice.   Wetness.
Tight vests   Leather
Hands; long fingers.
Heavy massage on buttocks
Wine
Tennis players bodies.
Initiating - being in control.
Backs of necks. Hard nipples.
Baggy jeans.
Anticipation. Slow dancing.
Smell of sunkissed flesh...

Turn Offs.

Lack of choice.
Pain
Words like tit or boob.
My head / hand being pushed down (wordless instruction.)
Nausea. Swallowing semen.
Not being relaxed.
Peoples pets in the bedroom.
Crumbs in the bed..
Thinking. Fear.
Hairy backs.
Using a cap.
Observing.
Fat beer guts
Doing things to me without thought...

thing is to begin to define for yourself what you like and don't like as a first step towards communicating some of these things to sexual partners. Communication will be discussed in Chapter 15.

The next step is to build your own cache of erotic materials. If this immediately conjures up an uninspiring vision of the average contents of a sex shop, think again! If women have been considered, it is usually women as men want them or expect them to be, not as they are. A perfect example of the latter is the inspiration behind the manufacture of the only readily available vibrators. They are shaped like penises and, functionally, the tip is not really conducive to adequate clitoral stimulation. Comfort and suitability to female anatomy had less impact on the design than the emphasis on vaginal penetration (see Further Information on page 181).

If we don't like what is available, we can create our own *personal erotica*. Women bring to class their erotic toys. These may be sensual objects, which feel or smell good, a piece of material, an old leather jacket, a favourite scent. They may be more explicitly sexual like naughty knickers or a vibrator or an erotic poem or a particular piece of music. With a growing awareness of our erotic potential, the simplest of objects begins to take on a different dimension – in this way, the erotic and sexual become much more integrated in our everyday lives. We begin to get away from the definition of sex as simply a matter of who puts what in which orifice.

With the permission and encouragement of a class, many women begin to experiment at home with different ways of expressing themselves sexually. This might be in painting or writing or even cooking (I've seen some *very* intriguing pie-crusts!). Sometimes, women experiment more with themselves; one woman had the wonderful idea of taping herself on a cassette recorder as she masturbated to orgasm and then played it back to herself while she relaxed and continued to enjoy herself in the bath – an open and honest statement of being sexual and enjoying it.

One task which each woman is asked to do is to write an erotic short story. The value of these is not necessarily the end product. The significance is the process of writing, which is a strong statement of each woman's own sexuality. Although we often fall into the trap of wondering, as ever, what impression it will make, it is important to write for our *own* enjoyment. There is no need to read them out loud but some women are happy to share their stories in the group. The experience of listening to these stories has always been inspiring. Given our cultural restrictions, I am convinced that this is one positive step towards establishing a sexual identity for ourselves.

Being able to design something erotic for ourselves in any medium confronts sexual dependence and passivity and shame.

When I was writing this book, I enquired of women I knew who had completed a sexuality course if they would be willing to have their erotic stories included. Understandably, many felt shy and reluctant. But twelve women sent me their stories, sometimes with the names changed to 'protect the guilty' as one woman put it! I was moved by the courage of this gesture and even more affected by the content. The stories reflect so simply and beautifully the actual experiences of women – these are not written by men for other men, they are written by women as a personal expression. Each woman speaks the truth for herself: the result is a combination of humour, poignancy and lust. Some of the stories incorporate fantasies, others reflect the reality of experience. As you read, remember these are ordinary women writing for themselves.

Story 1

'This way please, Ms Cameron,' said the receptionist as she ushered me in and handed my chart to the man waiting in the other room.

'Good day, Ms Cameron. How do you do? Do take a seat.' He studied my file. 'Good. Will you just slip off your clothes, Ms Cameron and we'll see what we can do.'

He began preparing himself over near his desk. I watched the back of his white coat as I undressed.

'Hmm. Good,' he said, turning round drying his already immaculately clean hands with a paper towel. 'Just hop up there will you, on your back first.'

I hopped up on to the couch and felt his hand sink deep into my belly.

'Good,' he said, steadying me with his hand. 'Comfortable?' His hand was burning into me and the heat was gushing through my body.

I sighed deeply. 'Yes,' I said, 'I'm fine.'

'I'll begin generally, just to check.'

I nodded and felt a sudden rush of sensation to my head in anticipation of what I knew must happen.

His hands began to brush lightly over my skin lingering at times over my neck, on my nipples, along the crevice of my waist and up over my hips, just the way I like it. As his fingers passed down along the soft skin of the inside of my thighs, I shuddered. It was happening again, I could no longer hold on.

'Good,' he said and then slowly cupped his hands over my breasts and began massaging them gently. I began to shake my head feverishly in an attempt to escape the burning heat. I felt the cool of his shadow over me. Beads of sweat ran down my face. My hair was wet and wild. He stopped. I moaned, feeling a violent drive from inside me, beginning to rise.

'Good, I'll just explore a little further. Don't be disturbed. I'll simply do what is necessary.' He smiled gently. 'You're doing fine,' he said as he bent over and bit gently into my right nipple and then began to suck furiously.

The fire within would no longer still. I began to writhe furiously. The sun seared through my body as his hand slid into my cunt. I knew my fight was over. I listened to the sound of his finger on my juices and his lips sucking at my breast. The sea lapped easily and I gave my body up and felt the wet of the water explore my body totally. I allowed it to embrace me as I floated and moved rhythmically in its power. He took his mouth away. His lips and mouth were wet. He licked his lips.

'Now, Ms Cameron, just another little while. This is the most important phase and I'd appreciate your cooperation.'

He went down to the end of the couch and began to stroke the inside of my thigh. My fire arose again, no respite.

'Flex your knees and allow them to fall out to the sides please.'

I obeyed and knew my cunt was fully open, ready and juicy. He stepped up on to the couch, straddled me across the waist and bent down, parted my lips with his hands and began to lick my clitoris and then my whole cunt. I heaved and threw my cunt up into his mouth. I flung myself from side to side but he held me fast and sucked. I felt him explore me deeper and deeper.

I screamed as the fire rose higher and higher until I was all aflame. For a second I looked up from the depths of my belly and a huge roar rose as the waves crashed down engulfing me, tossing and caring for me until I came to rest.

'Well done, Ms Cameron. I can see a definite improvement. When you're ready, you can get dressed.'

He was already vertical again with his immaculate white coat buttoned up. The sea abated, the sun cast longer shadows. It was late.

'I'd like to see you in a week's time. Please make an appointment with the receptionist on your way out,' he said smiling, handing me my chart.

Story 2
The sun caressed my naked body, the gentle breeze touched me while the grass and ferns played on my flesh. I was alone, yet not alone. The

trees, air, grass and sun kept me company. One with the earth, feeling part of it, I was at home.

This is where I belong, the clothes, buildings, structures of the man-made world have taken my freedom, myself, my right to be. I keep my sexual parts covered, for the sake of men who might lust after me, or even worse touch and fondle me.

I want to be with myself. Discover my own body, explore every part of me in relation to nature, find out who I am. I want to roll on the earth, touch the grass with my breasts, spread out my legs to take the warmth of the earth into my body. Grass and fern touch my vulva and my body is excited, the touch is gentle, so gentle.

Do I long for the touch of human hand or body? No, I enjoy the long grass, the fronds of fern that touch me so gently. I roll over hoping there is no bramble or thorn to pierce and scratch my bare flesh. I make love with the earth, slowly ecstatically, this is where I belong, I am home, I am happy, I wait.

Suddenly, without warning the earth takes me over, consumes me with passion. I want to bury myself in the long grass. Touch me, touch me more, I beg. I squeal with absolute ecstasy. Nothing could be more self-giving than this. I belong, I am part of something so much greater, bigger than I.

I subside into sleep, I dream, I love, I fondle, I touch, the sun through the trees warms and caresses my naked body. I am at peace.

Story 3

Candida once met a man for whom she immediately felt a physical feeling, something which happened to her very rarely, and with him she began a subtle erotic dialogue made up of gestures, looks and words.

The first real encounter happened once in the mountains. It was Christmas; the two of them were in a little mountain hut in the Val di Susa, they had gone there to rest, to enjoy the silence and those lovely landscapes made of valleys, mountains and snow. The hut was pretty, made of wood, with kitsch furniture. In the bedroom there was a fireplace where they lit a fire as soon as they arrived. It was so cold there that at first they didn't dare to undress. They both began to kiss each other slowly and to lick their foreheads, their eyes. She had the idea of licking his ears at length, first on one side then on the other, his chin, his neck, which she also gently massaged with feather-light fingers. They began to insinuate their hands into the covered parts of their bodies. The room began to feel a little warmer – or, excited as they were, they no longer felt the cold.

They were in no hurry to take off their clothes. Everything was done extremely slowly. There! Off with their pullovers, first hers, then his, their vests. They began to cover the naked parts of their bodies with kisses, caresses and licks. Their natural perfume contributed to their excitement. She said she wanted to make him a jacket of kisses and she set to work straight away, having the patience to cover every tiny area of his torso. She paid particular care to the 'pocket', over and over again. She then decided to make him another 'pocket' out of a sense of fairness and so she set to work on his other breast too. When she finished, he caressed her all over. He had a cream with him and he softly and delicately spread it over her, patting and stimulating every cell in her body. Her back got special treatment, made up of kisses for every vertebra and little touches so as to stimulate every nerve and bring new life to her. She then had the idea of putting a little Cointreau in his navel and sipped it and sipped it – until he moaned with pleasure. At last without a word and at the same moment they took off the rest of their clothes and finally naked they began to caress each other, beginning from below, kissing and massaging their feet, their calves, their legs; they reached the groin and they licked it, they still didn't touch each other *there*. After massaging and licking all over their bodies, he began to slide his fingers into her and she into him. They moaned with pleasure, stimulating, she felt she possessed him and was his source of pleasure, and he felt he possessed her and it was all like a merry-go-round of pleasure and love.

It may seem absurd but Candida's little finger placed right *there* gave him a strange pleasure he had never known before, that of being at the same time possessed and possessor. For her it was something beautiful, because she felt that every touch had its reply and nothing was hanging in the air. No exploration was forbidden, no area neglected. They never tired and when one of them felt the other about to come, they let go for a moment so as to increase tension and pleasure.

You know that the most beautiful thing a person can imagine is that which he will never possess. And so this interminable game went on, where instead they did possess each other but not completely, they knew how to wait so as not to use everything with a wrong movement. They were going on with this game when she, exhausted, stretched out beside him. At last he penetrated her. It was an immense pleasure for her, and her belly quivered in welcome to him. She squeezed him hard and he lay still and was excited just by the movement she was making. At last she asked him to change position, she wanted him to stretch out with her sitting on his penis. And so they went on still slowly without losing the contact that there was between them. He began to thrust forward and she gathered him in her grip and it was an indescribable pleasure for both of them; they felt their bodies quiver all over with it, every cell took part in their pleasure. At a certain point together, they began to shudder, they couldn't stop any more. At last the longed-for moment arrived, without any hurry, and it was sweet and interminable for both of them and it shook them. The summit melted away like snow in the sun and they, exhausted, let themselves go into this new kind of pleasure, so new, so complete, so different from the others, because it hadn't been a victim of haste and of taking everything at once.

Story 4

I phoned her at work from a call-box. She wasn't at her extension so I left a message. As I mouthed her name, my mouth dried. My heart pounded. I felt *ludicrously* nervous. But I had to do it.

We had been meeting in the same Spanish class every Tuesday evening for the past few weeks and I was quite beside myself. I fancied her so much that it had all become seriously out of hand. I was uncomfortably aware of trying to impress her and I hated myself. I was becoming obsessive; I couldn't talk to anyone about it so I kept fantasizing or pining like an adolescent. I decided that the only solution was to come out with it and tell her. Somehow I knew that if I could get it off my chest, the agony and turmoil would lessen and I could resume a normal life!

I phoned again. This time she answered. I heard myself calmly saying that I had something I wanted to talk to her about before we met next Tuesday. Could we meet that afternoon for tea? Yes. Fine. Four o'clock.

I arrived early at the café and sat there wondering what the hell I was doing! Through the window I could see her arrive and my first impulse was to hide. 'Hello,' I said nonchalantly. 'How are you?' We managed to chat about nothing at all for five minutes then I drew a deep breath. 'I have to tell you that I'm very attracted to you.' Pause: 'I don't want to do anything about it, don't worry. It's just that it is getting in the way of enjoying the class and so I wanted to tell you and have it out in the open. I hope you don't mind.'

I sat back and waited. I don't know quite what I expected but she was irritatingly cool and non-commital. After such a huge admission on my part, I felt the very least she could do was offer *some* kind of response. I asked for one. She said she felt touched and warm and that was all she could say. We talked a bit about ourselves and our lives and finished on a friendly note. It felt a little strange but I genuinely felt so much relief at having made my confession that I was positively euphoric as I kissed her goodbye on the cheek and climbed into a taxi to come home. I sat there reflecting that I had done the right thing and felt pleased that everything would be easier when we met again in class. Now I could forget about her and get on with my own life.

Half an hour after I got back, the phone rang. 'I've been thinking about what you said . . . I would like to see you again,' she said. 'Can I come round?'

Story 5   Taken by the Wind (a story with a multiple-choice ending)
This is the tale of a planned walk up the road to buy some bread; a

walk I do at least twice a week. Noad's have had a bread shop at the top of the road for over a hundred years and they make a very good nutty wholemeal loaf. It takes twenty minutes to walk from the house to the shop and back. I have a choice of ways I can go, I can go up one way and back another – up the road and round the drive or up and down the road, I never seem to go round the drive and down the road.

Going up Bloomfield Road I notice the cars and trucks and buses as it's a fairly busy road. Round the drive is very quiet, sleepy houses and not much moving and I can look at gardens and pop along the path that backs our gardens and take a quick peep over the wall to see if it's still there.

I go up the road – it's uphill from the gates. I can feel the wind on my face already. It's a fine sunny day, warm but windy, lots of big white clouds running across the sky. As I walk up, my hair blows back and colour comes into my cheeks and my button-through cotton dress blows tight against my body, encasing my legs and hard up against my breasts, so the shape is clear and I feel my nipples respond to the cool breeze and become alert and stand out through the cotton of my dress.

The wind gets stronger as I go on up the hill and for a while I'm engaged in the fight to keep my dress over my knees and my buttons closed, as my bodice is pushed and stressed by the wind. I feel excited by the warm wind between my thighs and under my arms and over my chest, breasts and my face. I feel both caressed by the wind and engaged in a struggle.

I'm aware of passing motorists and of them noticing me, looking and going their way. As I approach the brow of the hill I see a big red car slow down and stop and notice the driver lean over the passenger seat and wind down the window. I guess he's going to ask me directions.

At this point I meet the full power of the wind as I come up out of the shelter of the hill. I suddenly lose control and the buttons pull out of their holes and my dress is pressed past behind me and makes a train for my shoulders. I'm on top of the hill, walking into the wind, full bare frontal, and the motorist asks me the way to the Royal Crescent Hotel.

1. I clutch my dress in a frantic attempt to pull myself together, look down the hill in the direction of the most luxurious hotel in town and give directions.

2. I proudly propose that I go with him and show him the way.

3. I continue walking and give myself the pleasure of the full force of the wind on my body, on my breasts, big and firm, and alert,

pointing forward and the delicate, delicious breeze through my knickers entering my vagina, meeting my excitement. I feel very warm and energetic and I run on into the wind with my dress train flowing from my shoulders and my long body along the flat plateau of the hill-top. The traffic lights are green and I cross the top of the hill. I buy my warm just-out-of-the-oven loaf from Noad's and then walk leisurely with the wind behind me, back home along the drive looking at the gardens and remembering my exhilaration.

Story 6

I had been considering the idea for over a year but it had never seemed likely to happen. I had been fairly passive and had waited for him to make a move but now realized that if I didn't take some responsibility for initiating the encounter I would probably lose the opportunity.

We moved with the others to the lounge and I sat next to him. The next two hours were deliciously tantalizing. His fingers brushed my knees, my thighs, my back, while making conversational points. I didn't flinch from his touch but returned the pressure. Still, it was not certain – a little flirtation after good food and better wine is not unusual at these gatherings. But my body hungered after his and I could not believe that he was unaware. The warmth of my body centering on my cunt was delightful but I wanted more. Finally he suggested that we walk to the pier.

Outside it must have been cold at 2 a.m. but I felt no chill. In silence we walked to the pier, sexual excitement mixed with awkwardness. It was a clear night and the pier was silent and gently floodlit. At the tip of the pier, we stopped. I turned my back to look out to the sea and felt him approach. My body was taut, concentrating on the distance between us. I couldn't see him but was achingly aware of the exactness of the space. I turned and he leaned towards me. We kissed awkwardly, aware of the strangeness of each other but, as the desire grew, the awkwardness disappeared. Hand in hand and again silent, we returned to the hotel.

Once in my room, the charge dissipated. The niceties returned. I made coffee and we sat in chairs separated by a mile of mutual uncertainty, discussing politics.

Finally, in desperation – how cool I sounded! – I stated that I was going to bed and would be delighted if he would join me. I carefully removed my clothes and folding them, looking everywhere but at him, I climbed into bed and waited. He joined me and we lay against each other, flesh against flesh, skin against skin. Our hands explored, our eyes watched. Our bodies became engaged in a frantic touching almost outside our conscious control. His body was smooth and firm and his penis erect. I stroked the tip aware of its girth. I circled it between finger and thumb and imagined *this* penis penetrating my cunt. My wanting now was extreme and my arousal was intense. Every part of my body was screaming for him and my cunt was throbbing fully. Maybe I signalled my readiness or maybe it was obvious but he turned, lifted himself on top of me and smoothly and slitheringly entered me. I touched the lips of my cunt in wonder, feeling his hardness and my sticky wetness. It was almost surprising to me that my excitement was so extreme and had such an obvious physiological component. I felt no need to guide his movements – the speeding and thrusting felt so good. With my being centred in my cunt, I was able on another level to feel and enjoy his fingers – contrasting with his penis – gently tracing patterns on my face – and to feel and enjoy the texture of the stitched silky eiderdown.

I was high but a little shy and therefore unable to let go enough to come. I took a risk and asked to come on top – for me a fail-safe orgasmic device. He expressed pleasure that I could so request and for a moment we lay side by side. Then I raised myself above him and lowered my body, I suppose, but it felt like my cunt alone, on to his erect penis. The coupling was smooth and we moved together. My clitoris felt exquisitely at the centre of my being and it could only have been moments before I became aware that my being and my world had centred deep in my cunt. The rest of my body was sucked into this centre and I felt as a huge feeling eye seeing the world only through my cunt. Finally, it felt, but almost immediately it was, I came and came and came and came with feelings and throbbings centred on my cunt but generating to the tips of my fingers and toes.

We lay down quietly; only our fingers tracing those facial patterns and our eyes joined deeply. Still connecting through our genitals we moved together – my recovery was fast and I had the joyous experience of fucking and feeling and at the same time gazing out of the windows into the dawn, watching the sea crashing on the beach below. I shared this experience and was rewarded by his excitement. There was so much to explore between us and so little urgency to do so. Tiredness and warmth took over. We lay together and whispered and just lay and felt. Finally the sun came up and we parted to sleep. We were aware that in two hours we would be together as different, working people. I felt no regrets, it might happen again, there was no urgency, but what pleasure, what intimacy we had shared.

Story 7   Reclaimed Erotica

You are the most sensuous man I have ever met and I'll never forget your lovemaking. But, so that I don't, I'm going to describe it in detail here.

Your first kiss was sexual. Your tongue slid across my lips and into my mouth. I had intended just a friendly kiss: I was surprised, very surprised. You use your tongue everywhere, kissing my ears and neck, my nipples, arms and thighs. Licking me as you do, and of course, my cunt – but not that often.

The night you came back from France, though, my God, that was all we did: me sucking you off and you licking me out for hours and then a quick, very quick, fucking for you to come inside me. That's all you wanted, didn't give a damn about me, and you shouted as you did it – 'I'm going to come inside *you*.' It was as though that act symbolized something for you, though God knows what.

You aren't big. I've had bigger men inside me and not been half so satisfied. And you don't move a great deal or prolong the actual fucking. It's what comes before and afterwards that makes it so good. We reached orgasm together only once, yet I came every time. You'd stay in me and just press and press and press till I came. It was me who did the moving.

I think it surprised you when I made love to you the second time. I simply felt equal with you in bed and sometimes more than that, sometimes I despised you for your infatuation. I used to lick the inside of your thighs and you loved it. Every minute of it. And one night I actually hated you. I thought, 'You fucking communist party intellectual,' as I moved up and down on top of you with your prick inside me and, actually, it made me come. Perhaps that's the kind of trip that men are on – power.

Then there was the time when I couldn't stop coming. We were doped at the time and you called it a ... 'multi-media experience' and made me laugh, which you did a lot.

Perhaps it was because we were so alike that we made it so well together.

Your hands were beautiful, so beautiful. Fine-boned and small Jewish hands. And your beautiful Jewish face with impenetrable brown eyes and dark, dark curls – soft – and that tongue and sensuous mouth on my neck while you were inside me. It was, indeed, exquisite and intoxicating, like connoisseurs drinking fine wine.

Story 8   A Peak Experience
The night was hot and humid; the road rough and dusty. I wanted a

drink, a shower and a change of clothes. As I walked I could hear strains of music – jazz music. Now, for me, hearing jazz is like honey to the bee; a light to the moth; metal to a magnet – I am drawn. So I followed the sound. My path followed the stream through some woods and then I smelled the sea. The trees gradually thinned out, the music came clearer and I could hear voices. Suddenly I was there. Where?

On the beach of silver sand; its semi-circle gently meeting a calm navy-blue sea, where white frothy wavelets flowed and ebbed in light bubbles. The sky matched the sea's colour and countless stars gave their light in startling brilliance. A sliver of crescent moon shone softly over beach and sea. The sea reflected back that light in its own unique pattern; the beach accepted it.

People, naked, dark brown skin of the sheen that compares with no other; neither silk nor satin, petal or leaf; simply the lustrous sheen of human skin. People – meeting and parting with an ease and fluidity that seemed to match the sea's ebb and flow. Voices – rich and warm, sounds of laughter and delight. And the music – part of it all.

They played a music that was born of life; its joy and anguish, pain and delight, its sorrow and its glory, its harshness and compassion, its love, exuberance and spirit. My heart and soul met this music, dived and soared. The guitar alone unutterably poignant, then the drum, powerful and insistent, joins in; the piano, coming and going in a rapturous stream of known and unknown notes, the violin, reaching exquisite peaks of delight. The saxaphone now sultry, now seductive, soulful, bluesy, bawdy, urgent, longing, l-a-z-y; the flute, trilling crystal clear, soaring, the clarinet teasing. It was a jam session par excellence with a spontaneity and exuberance, a harmony and a joy that was tangible.

I lay back on the soft sand and absorbed each note through every pore. I closed my eyes.

Warm hands touched me, spreading aromatic oils on my hands and feet. Gently kneading my skin, one finger, then another, one toe, another. I felt every line, pore and nerve-ending being eased, caressed, tendered. I felt little beams of energy coursing through me and out in response to every touch. Each hair on the back of my hands and the tops of my feet, each pore responded. Not a bit of my skin was missed.

Sweet sounds from the clarinet.

Effortlessly and with instinctive ease each person moved up my body: wrists, ankles, calves, knees, arms, elbows, each fold and dimple, curve and hollow. Slowly I felt a release of erotic delight within me. Wetness flowed in my cunt, deep pulsings. Energy from every part of my body travelled to my cunt, my clitoris, and there was transmitted and intensified and radiated outward again. I uttered sighs of pleasure and moved my body to drink deeper the sensations. Sometimes their touch was light as gossamer, barely touching, another deep and strong. Hands caressed my face, ears, head, breasts, belly, cunt. My juices flowed. Fingers whispered at my nostrils and I breathed my cunt's pungent smell, fingers touched my lips and I sucked them in and tasted the creamy sweetness of my cunt, a penis delicately stroking my anus, a tongue at my ear, between my toes, titillating my clitoris. Music pulsated rhythmically into me and out of me. Smell, touch, taste, sound, I felt delightfully delirious. Sense of inside and outside melted. I laughed and groaned, sighed and squealed, moved and thrust, trembled and gasped. I bit, licked, nuzzled, kissed. My excitement mounted. Cunt kissing, being kissed, penis stroking and being stroked, nipples brushing thighs. Hands, arms, guitar, legs, mouths, saxaphone, clitorises, wetness, hair, cunts, drums, oil, sweat, penises, flute, tongues, ears, toes, clarinet – I lost track of what and who was there in a joyous exciting, erotic, sensual ballet and surrendered to it all, orgasm on orgasm in ultimate abandon.

Later, I danced. And what a dance! I'll tell you about that next time!

Story 9

I went to dinner at a friend's house. She said she had some interesting people coming round, 'You'll like them, Kay, they're just your type.'

I hadn't been there for many minutes when I realized just how right she was, certainly in the case of James. There was something captivating about his eyes, crystal blue and deeply set. A lot of chatter and pleasantries – all I remember of the pre-dinner conservation is holding James's penetrating stare.

How many people were there? Five? Six? We were placed either side of a table corner – so easy now not to just look and feel.

The soup was ankles and a gentle stroke of feet on feet. It was easier for me to slip off my shoes and as I slid my toe up his legs slowly, I held his eyes and circled my lips with my tongue in anticipation of what was to come.

The fish course found his hand gently stroking the inside of my thigh. I hadn't realized before the advantage of wearing a skirt on these occasions! As his fingers slowly moved upwards, my cunt grew hot and magnetic, but how he teased me – getting so close and yet not touching!

As our plates were changed, I slowly undid his zip, letting my hand gently caress the bulge of his penis. As I drew out the throbbing flesh, I thought 'Two can play at that game' and I toyed with the surrounding area, only occasionally letting a finger stroke up and over the top. With the dessert, we teased no longer. I felt his fingers inside my panties and explore my already wet slit. We built up quite a rhythm and the chairs and the table rocked. The room grew silent with enthralled fascination and as I reached the heights, he leaned right over and stifled my scream with the pressure of his kiss.

Story 10
   'I think that I would really like
   To be the saddle on a bike'

John Betjeman

'I'm off, love,' she shouted. 'I'll not be long – just the usual route.'

'Take care, then,' he replied.

It had been a bad day, the kids had been hell – but this was her hour of freedom. Cycling had become a kind of mental and physical therapy for her, a way of releasing all the pent-up tension inside, of regaining her sanity, enabling her to face another day. Each evening, if she could manage it, she cycled the same ten-mile route – sometimes she pushed herself really hard, knocking minutes off her previous time, other nights she took it leisurely, enjoying the long slow sensual pleasure of her legs pushing against the pedals, urging the bike along.

The fresh air, the wind on her skin, the sense of freedom as she sped along – all these combined, made the worries and niggles of the day fade into insignificance. This was her time, her chance to think, to be alone with her thoughts – and her body.

It was a warm summer's evening: one of those rare nights without a hint of chill, when the air is soft and balmy. She wore a tee-shirt and shorts, the sun was still warm and soaked her face and body. She cycled along country lanes. The sights and smells made her spirits soar. But especially the smells – the subtle scent of wild roses, a field of broad beans in bloom, applewood burning, new-mown grass .... She was getting into her stride now, the smooth action of her long brown legs, the breeze on her face, the saddle between her legs. She seemed to be part of the machine. The sensation was delicious – the slow smooth pressure of the saddle against her cunt felt like a lover's caress. She could feel the dampness in her shorts.

And then she sensed another rider beside her. A man in a black top and shorts, a fine powerful body in time with hers. Bronze-like limbs, tensing and straining against the pedals, strong brown arms gripping handle-bars. He never acknowledged her, he kept his eye on the road ahead, but he was in time with her. She caught the faint smell of his sweat on the breeze, saw the damp tendrils of hair on his neck and forehead. They seemed to be as one – the strong rhythm of his legs and hers – the panting of their breath. She felt the sweat between her breasts, the saddle between her thighs, the warm breeze on her legs. The pounding rhythm as they sped along the lanes. He never spoke and neither did she – to speak would shatter the magic. All her body was aroused, her nipples were firm and erect, her cunt was tingling. On and on they went, pounding, on and on, the rhythm getting stronger and stronger until suddenly . . . she came . . . the most intense orgasm of her life, like an explosion inside her, a dark flood of electricity through her body. She gasped. The man turned and gave a soft knowing smile and then sprinted into the distance. She nearly lost control of the bike but recovered quickly. She could feel the wetness and each time she moved in her saddle, a shudder of excitement ran up her inside.

She reached home a few minutes later – damp with sweat. Her cunt felt twice its size, swollen and warm and damp. She was breathing rapidly as she locked her bike away. A soft glow enveloped her body. She went inside. A voice called from the sitting room: 'Had a good ride, dear?'

'Yes,' she murmured quietly. 'Amazing!'

Story 11

I touched his back by mistake at a dance. He turned round. I said, 'Sorry,' and moved on.

I saw him coming towards me. We danced briefly. He wanted to leave, but I was scared. He wanted to stay the night. I said 'No.'

'Why?' he said.

'Because I have three children.'

'So what?' he said.

'I don't know if you'll be here tomorrow.'

'I will,' he said.

'Or next week?'

'I will,' he said.

'But I don't know that.'

'I will,' he said.

So I said, 'I'm scared.'

'In that case, the sooner you get it over with, the better.'

I found that acceptable, and suggested we moved to the bedroom.

He kissed me, and my body, and I felt his tongue on my cunt. It was exciting, it was tremendous, it was new, but it was wrong. I didn't know him. There were no feelings. Well, not enough for this!!

Wow!

He was above me, and inside me, and he was saying something. 'Tell me!' he said. 'Tell me!'

113

'Tell you what?'

'Tell me you can feel my prick up your cunt. Tell me you want to be fucked.'

I was really scared, but I said the words, as he moved his penis in and out.

Then he said, 'Come on top of me.'

'But I don't want to, I don't know what to do.'

'I'll show you,' he said. So I did.

After that, he turned me round and entered me from behind. Then he saw the mirror at the foot of my bed and looked in it. I was embarrassed. I didn't like what was going on, but didn't feel there was anything I could do.

Then he said, 'Now I'm going to come,' as though it was a decision. A few minutes later he withdrew and ejaculated over my back. I didn't like that, but I was glad because I didn't want his come inside me. I didn't know him.

After the shower, we went down into the kitchen and I made something to eat. It was comfortable listening to him chatting about his plans and I liked him, in spite of the bedroom experience. I enjoyed the easy way he accepted the food I gave him, as though he had a right to be there. I felt at home in my kitchen, in the atmosphere I had created, and he even talked about some additions he would like to make. I felt right with him and dismissed my dislike of what had just happened.

I said I wouldn't see him next day, I had work to do.

Next time we met he said he wanted exclusive rights. He seemed very direct and very honest and very powerful. I was confused. I wanted him but I didn't want what happened in bed. So I told him.

He never did those things again, and we didn't have sex very often. I couldn't understand it. If he was so experienced why didn't he want it more often? I did.

One night, long after he had the key to the house, long after we'd had good times, worse times and terrible times, he came in, in the middle of the night. He came in the dark, into my bed and put his arms round me. He fucked me. It never felt like making love.

I wanted him to kiss my neck, my mouth, my face and gradually move down my body. I wanted to feel his hands on my face, on me, on my body, in the petals of my cunt. I wanted him to be moving his face around the warmth and comfort of my thighs and resting there. I wanted him to know how special I was and that sex to me is an expression of love and not something I did just to have an orgasm. But the closeness never came. I felt alone. I couldn't find him. I didn't know where he was. He never used my name. I wanted him to share his feelings with me. I wanted to share mine. But we didn't seem to share anything except that the feelings were there.

I wanted to explore his body, and enjoy it. To become at home on him, in him, round him, with him. To feel warm and wet and equal. But it doesn't happen. I can't break through the barrier.

I give, he takes. Sometimes he gives – but we never seem to share.

So when I want to be with him, and he's not there, I get into bed and bury my head in his pillow where his after-shave lingers. Then I stroke my body, and feel the softness of my skin. I think about the curve of his hip, and the roundness of his bottom just behind me when we sleep. Then I wonder why he's not here when I want him – just to be here.

I think about how nice it is when I lie with him and rest my hand on his penis, and then he turns over and his head is above mine. I lie on his arm and push against him and that's how I sleep. But he's not here. So I stroke my cunt, and think about how it feels, and it feels good. I open my lips and gently move the clitoris round and round. I hear myself moaning and then as I get nearer to orgasm I imagine him as we were that first night, above me, thrusting, using the words and calling me babe. That stays with me until I've finished. I even hear the noise he makes when he comes.

After all, I feel peaceful and happy, mingled with sadness. There is joy to share. Why can't we share it?

Story 12   Fireflies and Moths
They saw the fireflies on their first evening returning from the taverna. They walked slowly along the path in pitch darkness, their arms rounding each other's waists in comfortable pleasure. Suddenly they stopped, both holding their breath at the wonder of those tiny globes of light darting back and forth in the blackness.

One woman said softly to the other that it was part of a mating ritual. They each silently noted that this augured well. The second woman was a lot more uncertain than her companion about many things in her life. She worried how it would be to spend three whole weeks on their own together. They hadn't known each other long – she had arranged this holiday many months ago but had agreed when her friend suggested that she should accompany her. She would always cherish the memories of that holiday.

The little villa was basic enough but the garden in which it stood was enchanted. Untidy, part-wild, part-cultivated, beautiful, colour-ful, unpredictable, constantly changing. It housed poppies and daisies and several small trees from which they picked lemons and oranges and kumquats. It was inhabited by an old and characterful tortoise and a stream of flying visitors – birds and insects whose sounds soon made them distinguishable as individuals.

There was so much to delight every sense. They made love everywhere. In the afternoon, lying on one of the creaking twin beds in the shaded bedroom, they would love and play for hours. She was amazed that her lover's fingers could always seem to find yet another small part of her vagina which was still ready for more pleasure. Kissing her lover's wet body in the shower early one morning, she tongued her way into the labial folds, both intently focused on each other until startled by the clatter of the toothmug as a small green frog took flight.

Occasionally a farmer and his donkey would pass behind the tall hedge and the travel agent dropped by a couple of times to make sure they had everything they wanted, but otherwise they were left undisturbed. So they were able to make a bold statement of their passion in the enchanted garden in the sunshine, their limbs extended wide, rejoicing in the freedom of it all.

She was ever open to her lover's lips and fingers – she was open and accessible as she had never felt before. For the first time in her life, she felt she could really trust. She had opened her heart to this woman: she had shown her tears and her rage. She had opened her mind to this woman – she had shared her thoughts, her ideas, her perceptions, her illogicality. And so she could open her body to this woman. She could trust her with herself. With her wildness, her untidiness, her cultivated pretensions, her beauty, her unpredictability, her changes.

There did not appear to be a specific beginning or end to their sexual exchange. It was more like a current of energy. They saw it like an erotic moth which would arrive quite unexpectedly and hover over one or both of them, imperceptibly triggering an impulse which took shape in an idea or a word or gesture.

She remembered its arrival one particular noon-time. She was standing wearing a loose shirt at the kitchen sink, cutting up beans for lunch, when she heard her lover come in and close the door. She began to melt a little as she felt long silky fingers under her skirt, stroking her buttocks up and down and around, getting more, then less, insistent. She felt one finger tracing a slow line from her cunt up through her crease. She felt her gut surge and she turned round. As soon as they kissed, they lost themselves in an intensity of motion. She arched her body to greet those long fingers which fucked her again and again, reaching deeper and harder. The two of them created the wave and rode it until it subsided. Dripping with sweat, they remained breathless, wordless, holding each other in harmony for a moment before opening their eyes and laughing quietly in surprise at what they had touched together. The moth flew on . . . but they knew it would be back.

Twelve women's stories: sadness, joy, sensuality, humour; the elemental, the powerful, compassion and hunger and, above all, the honesty and fun; multiple images of women as we are.

12

Tapping the Well-spring

Many women sense a connection between their own sexual experience and elemental forces, but with some apprehension. After all, it does sound bizarre! In a culture which promotes the joys of porno playing cards and crotchless panties or erecto-rams, associations with wind and waves or forests and valleys can feel a little out of place. And although it has long been acceptable for novelists like D.H. Lawrence to write evocatively of the relationship between sexuality and nature, when women come to express this for themselves, they are frightened by the power that the connection inspires and inhibited by the lack of language and lack of context. But the connection between women and nature is a very ancient one, and however commercial or mechanical sex has become we can reclaim a much broader and deeper sense of our sexuality for ourselves.

It helps if we begin to affirm for ourselves that sexuality is a part of the rest of our lives. We can acknowledge the erotic in everyday life without confusing it with sexual activity. It is difficult to remark on the erotic curve of an apple or the limb of a tree or a child's body or a flower or the sound of a musical instrument without being considered a little perverted. But it is the *being* of sexuality which we have lost in our obsession with the *doing*. We can experience a feeling of well-being after making love, but this is just one way. Our sexuality is a vital source of energy, which has no necessary connection with sexual activity. It is a well-spring in each of us, a spiritual and emotional resource within our bodies.

Sexuality extends far beyond the genitals, and sexual energy spreads throughout our bodies and throughout our lives. Women find what they call a new lease of life which is expressed in unexpected ways. One woman, a singer, found that her voice acquired a richer and deeper quality; another was inspired to take up sculpting again which she had left behind since she had married and had children. Others feel more alive and in touch with themselves. When a woman finds that her body belongs to her, the power she feels is unique. When she finds her body she finds her sexuality – and her own way of expressing it. In a group context, this gives rise to all sorts of experiments with creative forms – using clay or paint or dance or even theatre.

Celebration

Because so much of the process so far has been specifically concerned with looking, touching, enjoying and trusting our bodies, we spend some time together naturally – without our clothes. The barrier to removing those clothes is inevitable because we still fear criticism. We still feel inadequate and, even if getting undressed in front of others at a sauna or on a beach is no problem, this is different. Here there is no competition or comparison and no hiding. But the context is safe (and warm!) and we follow a rhythm which suits everyone. After that first hurdle, the actuality is wonderful. When we show what we are like, with all our variations of shade and texture and shape, we discover that our natural splendour quite overshadows the clothed versions! There is a lot of curiosity and permission to look and to appreciate. Above all there is a fascination in seeing our bodies as they really are rather than pretending or hiding or conforming to a mythical image.

One of the celebratory and healing rituals in a group is for each woman to take her time to be a 'goddess' with the other women being her devoted 'attendants' – restoring a sense of wholeness and grace to her body through their hands. The room is lit only by the flames of an open fire or candles; it is filled with occasional low murmurs and the smell of assorted fragrant oils. Women are together in threes or fours – one of them is lying on her back or her front being massaged by the others.

Watching the kaleidoscope of images – the variety of shapes and contours, some muscles flexed with effort, some soft and relaxed, a dance of movement and rhythm, there is a wordless chant of concentration and stillness, of giving and taking and I am reminded of the vitality and unadorned beauty of women's bodies. There are echoes of something very old and primeval, some ancient presence which cannot be described too clearly. And yet it is there – the profound sense of a still and magnificent power.

Bridges

If this were a story, it could end here. It might have been enough to have discovered that we are sexual beings in our own right and to have drawn strength from reappraising our attitudes and pruning unnecessary beliefs in the light of information and experience. We could survive with a glimpse of what it means to inhabit our bodies with pride. But in order to take that first look at ourselves, we have temporarily had to shut out the 'others', whether those others are at home or at work or in the street. We have had to put them aside for a while, otherwise it would have been impossible to maintain a single-minded focus on our own sexuality when we are so easily swayed by what others want or admire or expect.

However, reality demands that we be ourselves in the context of our everyday lives. Even if we are clear about ourselves, how are we going to incorporate those changes into relationships? Here we are most vulnerable because we feel our sexual and personal viability depends on the presence or absence of a partner. And because of this dependence, we are wary of each other when it comes to sharing concerns about relationships. It is difficult to avoid comparison and competition, and easy to slip into the trap of feeling sorry for or inhibited by other women.

Instead of comparing status, we can remember that whatever our individual differences, we have much in common. Whether or not a woman is in a committed relationship, she will find her own sexuality confronted every single day. None of us, celibate, single, widowed, married, divorced, living alone, with or without a sexual partner, can avoid sexuality as an issue in our general interaction with other people. Quite apart from chosen intimate relationships, we are confronted with it in many areas of our lives. A woman can feel affronted when the man repairing the cooker feels at liberty to stroke her arm; she can feel embarrassed when a colleague remarks on the size of her breasts; she can feel uncomfortable if a passenger on the train presses his thigh against hers; she can feel deeply upset by the intrusion of an obscene telephone call; she will feel more alert to the possibility of danger of she recognizes the shadowy figure in a dark street to be a man. Even without a male sexual partner, a woman cannot avoid a male perspective.

Holding on to our integrity is a struggle for all of us simply because we are alive today. How can we interact with others, with the real world, within a culture which is constantly undermining our ability, as women, to see and hold ourselves and our bodies intact? Starting from a point of self-acceptance can help us to be intimate without being swamped and swamping. It can help us to find a balance. Moving across the bridge from a position of clarity and strength is very different from rushing over to the other side in loneliness and desperation! A clearer personal definition of sexuality allows us to look with a different perspective at the way we interact with the others in our lives.

Most men find it difficult to talk to each other honestly about sex. Adolescent and young adult men gain some useful information on technique from peers, but a lot of what is exchanged is *mis*-information. As adults, men do not honestly discuss sexual problems or fears. Since much of what is said on the topic is designed to impress, many men find it impossible to admit to being anything less than the perfect sexual male. Although men generally may be familiar and fairly well informed about their own sexual anatomy and physiology, they know little about what goes wrong, about emotional matters or about the needs of women.

We have seen that a woman's sexual experience is an integral part of her experience of being a woman at every level in her life. In the same way it is meaningless to try to understand a man as a sexual being without reference to the culture from which he comes. This is not to say that all men see things in the same way, but there are clear cultural messages which many men will recognize.

Being a man. The messages about the necessary qualities of being a man are effective at every level of his life. The keyword of his social training is *mastery*. Mastery applies to all situations, his feelings, his body, any challenge that comes his way. For this he will need qualities of strength, invulnerability, a capacity for action and an urge towards achievement. From an early age, he will be encouraged to use his body, to be rough with his body, to extend its limits, push himself, to exert and extend his physical capacities. He will be encouraged to take knocks without showing they hurt. He will learn to show aggression in the face of fear. The urge to be master of himself and his environment propels him throughout his life because, like the vast majority of men, he will not believe he has attained this ideal. He will continually 'push harder' to 'do better' in order to assuage the nagging sense of failure in his image of himself.

Strength, invulnerability, action and achievement are qualities necessary in his sexual behaviour as well. He will probably learn that sex is secret and naughty and powerful and, like his sister, he will receive very little real information or facts. But, unlike his sister, he will probably masturbate, even if guiltily. He may well joke about it with his mates, be taught by one of them how to do it or compete to produce the highest spurt in the school urinal. He will handle his genitals with familiarity and ease. He may be startled when he first ejaculates if he hasn't been told what to expect, but with practice he will recognize the sensations in his penis and that, with some kind of stimulation, he can increase those sensations until they reach a climax, after which the sensations reduce their intensity. This sequence becomes the blueprint for future sexual behaviour.

In puberty he may suffer embarrassment about the frequency or unpredictability of his erections. He will be aware that it sticks out and gets in the way and that this part of his body is extremely vulnerable. But the vulnerability won't be mentioned. Instead the focus will be on the powerful aspect of its size and function. He will become aware at school of the importance of his penis – the bigger the better – and may worry if he believes his penis to be too small. He will learn that this is the central piece of equipment in adult manhood.

He will be expected to sow his oats, to gain experience. His sexual experiments will be accepted and often encouraged. Well before puberty he will have learned that a man has to get a woman. Why? Because like making money or moving mountains, sex presents another challenge. But, unlike the acquisition of money or the removal of obstacles, the achievement felt in sexual success has no tangible form, and although he will learn that sex can be a commodity, it is one about which he will develop a very deep ambivalence. This ambivalence – love and hatred of the same object – he will see mirrored in the stereotypes of male sexual behaviour towards women in the media, at school, at work, perhaps in his own home.

It is important not to underestimate the effect of the beliefs about sex handed down in the religious and social dogma of the past centuries. Remember, sex was seen as a monster with a terrifying power, which, if unleashed, could bring damnation and physical and spiritual destruction to all mankind. Remember, the face of this monster is female, its shape is female, its wiles are female.

As historical tradition feeds the imagination the man approaches this monster with caution. He fears its power to render him a helpless victim of his own body. Its face, its body, its cunning will plant the seed of desire which, as it grows and pushes for emergence, will overwhelm him and leave him vulnerable to spiritual death. His body was part of hers once – he was part of her flesh. He is reminded of his own helplessness, his nakedness, his own mortality. So, like any other threat, man must master this force he has been told is uncontrollable.

There is also a material and social dimension to this fear. Many men work on the assumption that what women want from them is love and security which, of course, many do. Meeting this need carries a price, both financial and emotional, that men do not always want to pay. Fear of being asked to pay encourages an exploitative and casual attitude towards sex and towards women.

If we look at some of the male sexual stereotypes in western and other cultures we can see how they often reflect different strategies for dealing with female power. First, there are those which revolve round the theme of man as **Predator**. His tool is violence. He appears as the Rapist, the Groper, the Flasher, the Seducer, the Pederast, the Sex Fiend.

In order to escape the enslavement of sexual arousal, but being helplessly drawn by his body's needs, the Predator must establish power over the source of fear: he must find a victim before he is one himself. He wants sexual satisfaction but does not want to pay the price. The Rapist must penetrate or kill, the Groper must seize and attack the most offensive parts, the Flasher must intimidate his prey by exhibiting his own alarming weaponry, the Seducer must aggressively contaminate the innocent with guilt.

In the second cluster of sexual images, the characters do not resort to outright attack but to exploitation. This is man as the **Operator**. He knows what to do – he is cool, shrewd. His tool is control, with which he can meet his sexual needs and still avoid a woman's physical and emotional demands. He knows every trick in the book for turning a woman on and bringing her to grateful ecstasy. He is controlled and controlling. There is the old smoothie, Don Juan, who believes he is God's gift to women, less ruthless than the true Operator but no less charming. And the Notcher who records his conquests with the same short-lived sense of triumph as a man who bags pheasants. There is the Sexual Athlete, whose antics are endlessly depicted in popular magazines, in porn and semi-porn. He has irresistible charm, which draws women helplessly to him, only too eager to open their legs for him. He can pick and choose among them and will discard what he doesn't want. He has sex on *his* terms.

There is also a more domesticated version, called the Rollerover, selfishly focused on having his own way, giving her one. No nonsense and no finesse – in, he comes, out, he goes . . . to sleep or back to his wife. Sex without an emotional price.

The third model offers another way of overcoming the monster, burying it. This is man as **Avoider** – his tool is repression. One stereotype is the monk, the spiritual ascetic who successfully denies his body's desires and everything which emerges from them. He has found that transcendence is the only answer to salvation. He repudiates all sexual pleasure and pursuits of the flesh, and in this way masters his own weaker self.

These models are not positive. Like the female stereotypes in Chapter 3, they are extremes which can become reality in some individuals' behaviour. But, for most men, they remain as images, powerful enough to influence ways of thinking and feeling, powerful enough to affect what men expect of themselves in and out of bed. These beliefs will probably be shared by their sexual partners, whether men or women.

These messages remain shrouded in half truth. They are hardly ever discussed openly, so we never find out just what is real and what is imaginary. Men certainly find it almost impossible to talk about the truth among themselves – there is so much at stake in continuing with the myth of mastery. Sometimes the acknowledgement of these myths can help us to understand just how much we are pressurized by our culture and to be able, in the light of this, to make up our own minds. In a women's group, women are able to see that their own experience does not necessarily match up to the stereotype – men can do the same.

Images and reflections

What are some of the messages about male sexual behaviour?
Predator. From this picture, the following messages emerge:

A man has urgent sexual needs.
A man is an animal.
Men are only after one thing.
A man is always ready for sex.

A man is a machine.
Man is a beast.

These messages affect behaviour in various ways.

'A man's got to do what a man's got to do.' A powerful message which affects men's experience is the deep conviction that a man's sexual needs are overwhelmingly urgent. Certainly, he may feel his sexual need for satisfaction to be urgent, especially when younger, and he may experience a powerful physical desire for satisfaction, but there is no physiological evidence to suggest that if he doesn't ejaculate he will do himself internal harm. But there is a tendency to exaggerate this urgency so that a woman is coerced, however subtly, into cooperation.

Many women would not entertain the idea of saying no to sex when not in the mood because they believe a man's sexual need is a matter of life or death! It is impossible to reach an assertive compromise between two equal individuals when one of them believes that her refusal to cooperate will result in dire consequences for the other. In addition, men's general reluctance to use masturbation as an option and to take charge of their own situation further reduces the possibility of equal negotiation.

'Look what you've done!' A touch or insinuation or a glance can all be blamed for starting something which has to be finished. Some men really do believe this. Many more women believe it. This assumption makes it twice as difficult to set honest sexual limits when a woman feels that she is responsible for the man's erection. She will easily feel guilty and agree to go ahead and get it over with to alleviate the guilt a little. She may well feel this without any encouragement, but if the man actually accuses her of this when he is aware that an erection can be produced by a whole variety of circumstances, it is no more than a con!

'Always just one thing on my mind.' Men often believe that they should always be ready for sex, i.e. for intercourse, and that to pass up an opportunity when it's on offer is unmanly. Turning sex down is tantamount to ducking out of a challenge. This encourages a lack of recognition of other valid needs besides sex, such as the need for physical closeness. It can also make it difficult for a man to say no to sex when he doesn't feel in the mood: he still feels he ought to make the effort.

Operator. From the second group come some more messages:

A man must perform.

A man must initiate.

A man must orchestrate.

A man is responsible for the success of a sexual interaction.

A man must be active.

A man must take charge.

A man must know what, when and how to do everything.

A man must know about sex.

A man must always be in control.

From these messages another theme emerges in relationships.

'*How did I do?*' Many men feel responsible for a sexual encounter with a woman. And, in wanting to please a female partner, a man may well feel assessed on his performance. Because communication is usually minimal, he can only go on what he believes she will want. Even if she doesn't want an orgasm, she is going to have one because he knows that this is how any successful encounter should end. He cannot ask for information because this would be an admission of ignorance. Very few men understand women's bodies any more than women do, and because the man has to keep up an image of assurance, he can well continue to grope in the dark from adolescence to old age.

It is not helped by female partners who *expect* a man to know what he is doing, *expect* him to take responsibility, *expect* that if he loved her enough, he would know how to please her, and who have no intention of communicating directly what they do or don't want. If a man does try to change the pattern and asks his partner to initiate, he may well meet with resistance from her for the same reason. Women can be too afraid of rejection to make a first move: they may be less coercive, because they feel less permission to have an 'urgent' need.

Of course, sometimes the messages can dovetail: if a man is in charge and his female partner enjoys him being in charge and is happy to let him have his way with her, all well and good, but there are times when problems emerge. He may not want to initiate – he may not know what he is doing. He may cover up his ignorance by staying with the routine. He may also find it very difficult to show vulnerability if his partner wants him to remain strong and manly. All in all, having to match up to the 'Operator' is an awesome challenge and one which makes many men feel inadequate.

Avoider. The messages from the third image strike an even deeper chord and engender fear and mistrust.

Men should not care.

Men should not get close.
Men shouldn't enjoy their bodies.
Flesh is dangerous.
Feelings are dangerous.
You must control by cutting off.
Beware of involvement.
A man must not show tenderness or vulnerability.
A man must not receive or be passive.
A man must not show fallibility or weakness.

'*No heart, no hurt.*' The only way to control is by keeping everything within very narrow confines. Along with repression of the body goes repression of emotions and repression of sensuality – anything which could be overwhelming. Being masculine is keeping it under tight control. Tenderness, receptivity and sensitivity to feelings – the human qualities seen as feminine – are inhibited.

Men can fall foul of expectations and mythology when they refuse to consider their own feelings. The learned need to hide vulnerability and the softer part of their natures has meant that many men have become unaware of their emotions and are unable to identify or understand their significance. Feelings can interfere with their sexual response, as happens with women. Because emotional issues are dismissed, men do not always recognize that if they cannot 'function', then it is because their bodies are telling them something that their heads will not attend to. This situation is aggravated by lack of clear information about the facts of male sexual response.

Men and sexual response

Men, like women, are prone to false assumptions about their bodies. This is further reinforced by silence and the belief that a man should know what he's about anyway.

The physiology of the male sexual response cycle follows the same basic patterns as the female cycle described in Chapter 7. The same process of arousal, the build-up of blood in the pelvic area, accumulation of sexual tension and the release in orgasm. There is a lot of available information about the physiology of male sexual response and Bernie Zilbergeld's book (details on page 183) is a very useful guide to men and their sexuality. So, for the purposes of this book, I will concentrate on what men are often interested and surprised to learn about themselves.

Arousal and erection. The processes of arousal (the desire for sexual stimulation) and erection (the penis filling with blood) are two separate processes, but they so often go together that we have come to think of them as one and the same. They are not. They are linked to different parts of the central nervous system and can operate independently of each other. It is only when something 'goes wrong' that we see this clearly. A man can feel aroused and strongly attracted to a partner and want to make love but be physically unable to get an erection. Another man may get an erection without being particularly focused on any one person or any specifically sexual activity.

The first point to note is that men cannot control their erections by will-power alone. Remember that the arousal process in a woman is triggered by all sorts of stimuli – some sexual and some non-sexual. This applies to a man as well. So he may have an erection in response to a sexual stimulus but an erection can also be produced by relaxation, warmth, memories, certain tactile sensations and other kinds of excitement. This can mean that a man might get an erection without consciously wanting sexual contact but, once produced, the sensations are usually pleasurable and produce sexual desire. For many men, and women, the erection of the penis is a signal of readiness for action which means continuation to orgasm. The powerful cultural message persuades a man that not to continue by fucking and reaching orgasm inside a vagina is less than manly. In reality, not to continue would not be a tragedy but merely a temporary physical discomfort.

Although the pelvic congestion and accompanying desire could easily be resolved by masturbation, many men dismiss that option because they believe masturbation to be childish: something done by boys who have not yet learned how to fuck and how to 'make it' with a woman. Resorting to masturbation becomes therefore an admission of not being a fully-fledged man. This emphasis also means that when a man does want to make love to a partner and his penis doesn't become erect, he can feel let down by his body and feel himself to be a failure.

The process of arousal can be blocked by the side-effects of drugs used in medication and many GPs are neglectful about giving adequate warning. It can be blocked by illness, by injury to the spinal cord, by alcohol, by fatigue and especially by feelings. By sadness – for example, at children growing up or separation or the upheaval of a divorce; by anxiety or worry about work or lack of it, coping with financial problems, uncertainty about the future; fear of losing a partner, fear of illness; frustration about work or home-life;

resentment towards a friend or someone in the family, anger towards a partner. All sorts of present worries and concerns interfere with a man's sexual arousal, as do deeper feelings from the past. These signs can indicate that all is not well but, instead of seeing their value, many men feel devastated by an inability to perform and, because they are afraid, will often blame a partner or their bodies for letting them down and not working on demand.

Misunderstandings can also occur when an erection is produced in a non-sexual situation – for example, when a man is hugging a friend or being massaged. This may well happen because of closeness, relaxation or sensual pleasure. Instead of realizing this is a response to various pleasurable stimuli, the erection has become linked with a readiness to fuck and it is assumed that the man must have only that *one thing in mind*. If the situation is appropriate, he and his partner may continue to the next move but if it isn't, the other person – a woman or a man – may be frightened or offended or outraged. He might well be embarrassed which can make it more difficult for him to handle the situation.

Assumption versus choice. If a situation like this ends in disaster, it is usually because neither party sees the possibility of any choice in the matter. It is difficult to accept that he can *choose* to seek sexual satisfaction with the person present or someone else or resolve the residual discomfort through masturbation. Or he can, as many do, learn to concentrate on a non-sexual image or thought which will cause the erection to subside. If a woman can accept that an erection in itself isn't an accusation or an order, she too can make a choice for herself. Guilt leaves her open to blackmail, whereas choice makes it a lot clearer for everyone concerned. Otherwise it is easy for the pattern to continue: an erection occurs, the interpretation follows, she feels guilty, he has to have release and the 'inevitable' happens, fulfilling the assumption and reinforcing the myth.

Men looking at women

Before we can explore some of the issues which emerge in sexual relationships between men and women, it is important to understand the often overlooked connection between social and sexual attitudes and expectations. How is a man encouraged to view a woman, his prospective sexual partner? Whether or not a man chooses to relate sexually to women, he will be aware of the heterosexual norm. How will he see his social role in comparison with hers?

As a boy looks at adult males, he will develop a clear sense of what is expected of him and what life holds in store. His future role will include the functions of provider, protector and achiever. The extent of his achievement will depend on his colour and class but, whether advantaged or disadvantaged, he will usually see a wider range of opportunity than does his female equivalent. All around him, those in charge are men. If he sees how women defer to men he will come to believe that to be his right as well. He will come to know that men are more important in the world and, even in an uncertain climate of future employment, he will be assured of more concern than his sister.

He will see and believe that male is the superior gender: past and present achievement, whether artistic, scientific, poetic, athletic, political, military, technical, commercial, literary, entrepreneurial or spiritual, is associated with people of his gender. Those in educational, legal, penal and governmental authority are generally men – all this gives a fairly clear idea of who's who and what's what in the world. With the tradition of the mother in the home, the woman's sphere of achievement is undoubtedly the domestic and he will soon be aware of how much those maternal and emotional spheres are valued.

Women don't count for much, they do the boring jobs, the trivial tasks – the things that no one else wants to do at home. His mother will probably make it clear that he is important – she may well treat his father as more important than herself. She's not much of an equal in other ways so how will he see her sexually? A man is encouraged to see a woman's body as an object from an early age. Even when a son feels close to and loved by his mother, offering a positive basis for future relationships with women, he cannot remain unaffected by the culture – portrayed in newspapers, television, in the magazines in the sweetshop. He may feel an uncomfortable conflict – why are bodies like his mother's and sisters' displayed in this way? He can see how women are treated and how they treat their own bodies – very much concerned with display. He learns the jokes about sagging breasts or large bottoms or fat legs. He will pick up the repulsion and the obsession.

He will feel encouraged by his mates to assess each part of a woman's body as she walks down the street or into a room. He is encouraged to touch what he wants to touch, usually unchallenged.

He will learn that 'pulling a bird' brings status among his peers and he has long been conditioned to value the opinions of his peers – because his status as a male depends on their opinions.

One way in which he can cope with the stress caused by this contradiction between love for a woman (his mother) and scorn for women's bodies in the world around him, is to construct a model of his mother as non-sexual, while other women can remain sexual and available. Another way is to cut himself off from the feminine part of himself – from compassion, emotion, flexibility and receptivity. If he marries and becomes a father himself, he may be able to love his wife as he once did his mother, but he may find it easier to get sexual titillation and satisfaction outside his home.

He can find it difficult to see a woman as a whole person. And yet he reveres the female body – he longs to fall in love, to feel that helplessness again, that obsessive need and enchantment. He enjoys the romance but then he finds out that this goddess has flaws – she's human. He may find it difficult after that to see a woman who is sexually available as a complete person in her own right.

It is clear from the sexual stereotypes that women's bodies have the power to attract and seduce men. The message is that women's bodies are objects of beauty and danger which must be handled appropriately. The Avoider is quite clear that the woman's body must be hidden – she is a potential temptation. The Operator sees her as an object of prey – he can enjoy the excitement of stalking his prey and the thrill of conquest. In this way, the power is harnessed for his enjoyment, like a fast car or, with more subtlety, a fine instrument on which he can play his own tune.

The Predator has to attack a woman's body. She is dispensable, her body provokes or invites attack by its very nature: it is her body which, in reality or fantasy, calls forth the monster. Which is why sexual assault, sexual harassment, battering, rape and murder will still be treated with complacency. There is an unspoken assumption that suggests that a violent release is inevitable, not very nice perhaps, but that women ask for it often enough, and if they didn't dress that way or walk down that road they wouldn't get themselves into trouble.

This attitude changes only when she belongs to another man. Then there is true outrage – after all, even a predator must play by the rules and keep to his own territory. But if she doesn't belong to another man, then she's pretty much up for grabs – after all, someone has to be the victim and isn't she to blame for all the trouble in the first place?!

Women looking at men

How does a woman collude with this? She has known for a long time that men were better, more interesting than women. She has long been conditioned to value the opinions of men because her status as a female depends on their opinions and acceptance. But male sexuality is confusing and frightening and exciting, often bestial and urgent and powerful. The only way for a woman to manage this beast is to surrender or to construct her own power games. She knows that men want 'it' and she knows that she has got 'it' and as long as she has got 'it', he will want 'it'. Consequently since she isn't anything without him anyway, she'll be able to hang on to him.

Sex becomes her highest priced commodity – one which she can bargain with. She is not interested in her own body for herself but in its power to attract – she puts a lot of energy into this, into flirting with the beast within, enjoying putting him down occasionally, enjoying the power of saying no, of seeing him in need and needing *her*. The shame about her own vagina, about being a woman, is temporarily alleviated – his penis inside her confers status, acceptance, power, beauty, validity – he makes her feel a real woman.

Therefore she needs a real man. 'Real' becomes equated with rough. The fatherly image is protective and benign, the brotherly image is friendly and affectionate but these qualities don't make a man *exciting*. She dismisses the nice, vulnerable, concerned, easy-to-talk-to man as unattractive and, if he doesn't make advances, concludes he must be homosexual. She wants a man to show that he is made of stronger stuff. This is what the fantasy promised would be her destiny.

Even if she doesn't always actually like the way men touch her or look at her, she doesn't like to say anything. After all, 'boys will be boys' and at least it means she's still got something going for her. She knows that inside he doesn't match up to her ideal – he's really pretty feeble, quite human in fact. In her disappointment and anger, she matronizes him: since he isn't bigger and better, he is obviously weaker. He can't cope with her feelings, or the truth, or change, or with cooking his own meals, so she has to protect him from reality. She lets him *think* he's boss, but she knows who's the real boss, doesn't she?

An interesting exchange takes place. He attributes her with beauty and sexual power. He then sets out to make it his. She feels a lack of beauty and sexual power until she feels it restored by him. This becomes one of the basic dynamics in the struggle for power in sexual relationships.

After-effects

Of course, sexual relationships between men and women are also about love and care and sharing and commitment and friendly intercourse at all sorts of levels. However, when problems arise, we all too easily turn to the mechanics to find the source, when most difficulties in sexual relationships occur because of cultural pressures and expectations. For example, the most common root of sexual problems in women stems from lack of arousal caused by anxiety and inhibition in place of understanding and self-acceptance. Similarly, many sexual problems among men stem from anxiety and inhibition imposed by cultural learning.

Detachment. It is hardly surprising that most information about men's sexual problems centres around the penis: either he cannot get an erection or his erection isn't hard enough or he comes too quickly or finds it difficult to come at all. Once again the culture equates a man's sexuality solely with the function of his penis. Certainly his penis is important, but the problem lies in the fact that the line between the penis and the heart has been broken. Since the penis has become detached from the heart, sex has become detached from care – both care for self and care for others.

The most common and severely disabling problem which men face in sexual relationships is the inability to be intimate. The message that a man must not be vulnerable has been extremely effective, so that many men have forgotten how to feel or how to express their feelings. They do not trust anyone, male or female, to explore their emotions and this emerges as a barrier to intimacy between men and men and between men and women.

Many women who are happy enough with the 'sex' find being locked out, being excluded from closeness, very isolating. And it isn't just a question of learning to cry, though it is a huge and important step for many men to acknowledge tender and compassionate feelings and to lay down the tough male mask.

Fear. The most elusive emotion for men is fear. Even men who have involved themselves in current movements which encourage the expression of feelings and who have learned they can give themselves permission to cry, can rarely touch their fear.

A man is vulnerable to a deep fear linked to the constant push to be master of himself, his body, other people, the world. The fact that mastery is impossible ultimately, simply increases the fear of exposure. This is compounded, in many men, by a deep mistrust of women, so the fear remains locked away and emerges only as aggression.

Loss of sensuality. With the penis so much in the spotlight, the significance of the rest of a man's body has been overshadowed and, with it, his potential for sensual, not only sexual, pleasure. Although there are two separate drives in human beings – for sexual satisfaction and for human closeness – men are more familiar with the former. It is difficult for a man to acknowledge a need for touch and closeness or a desire for tactile comfort when he pays so little attention to the rest of his body and when closeness risks being intimate! Asking for a hug on its own is often difficult, not only because it means acknowledging a need and facing rejection but also because of complications which may arise! If he does reach out and feel close, this might trigger an erection, so he may end up going through the motions of sexual activity just to get the human contact he wants.

When a man honours and acknowledges his own needs for touch and sensuality, he can begin to share this more with a partner. Many, many women complain that they want more physical contact with men but that, if and when they ask, men say they don't see the point or are very wooden and grudging or will only consider touching as foreplay, as a prelude to 'real' sexual activity. As long as the need for closeness is ignored and vulnerability avoided, this will continue to be an enormous barrier to intimacy.

Can any of this change? The main obstacle is men themselves. The majority of men are not interested in exploring this area because they are not interested in changing the status quo. Some men are motivated to change because they feel excluded by the changes in their female partners. Some may attend a course in sexuality because it is part of a professional training. A few men will seek help when something appears physically wrong with their ability to perform.

But very few men are interested in exploring this area voluntarily with other men. This is partly because many heterosexual men feel a lack of emotional closeness with other men. This has evolved through a pattern of traditional lack of fathering in the home, associated with a lack of attention, lack of touch, lack of emotional support, lack of warmth from men. And, of course, there is fear. Fear of becoming vulnerable by admitting to being less than master and, with such a strong heterosexual preoccupation, fear of other men as sexual predators.

When I have worked with men in a context of a sexuality group, I have always been moved by the power of honest exchange. It takes time and the mistrust has to be cleared but when men finally stop relating to each other emotionally through a woman, they can stop rationalizing their emotions, they can stop competing with each other, and can acknowledge fear non-aggressively. Then they can begin to be close to each other, which goes a long way to breaking the mutual dependency.

Men can construct a positive model of male sexuality. The penis, which has come to symbolize prowess, status and oppression, can be reintegrated as a loving and vulnerable part of their bodies. If men could reclaim their own beauty, their own skin, their own sensuality, their own vulnerability, then sex would be more of an exchange and less of a competition.

Anger is a powerful force behind many women's move to change; anger at feeling imprisoned inside a dummy body for so long, at having a body which has been so fragmented and bruised that they want to reclaim it for themselves. A lot of that generalized anger is expressed personally. It emerges both directly and indirectly, above and below the belt, in sexual relationships. Whether at the receiving end of an assertive request or outright hostility, many men are fearful of exposure, of change, of rejection. This increases defensiveness, and so we just don't listen to each other.

Fear of change affects us all, and in the current climate of uncertainty about future employment, or any future at all if the militarists have their way, fear is rife. Because roles are changing and consciousness is shifting, all of us feel more afraid – but men rarely give themselves permission to show this. Only when men can admit to and express their fear, can they really change. With understanding, information and sharing, men can mend the broken line between the heart and the penis. A fuller understanding could affect all a man's emotional relationships – as friend, lover, husband, brother, father – as a man and human being in this world.

Following on

1. You may have recognized some of the myths about male sexuality. It is helpful to review how you collude with these myths in your own relationship(s). For example, do you expect a man to know what he is doing in and out of bed? Do you feel disappointed or rejected or resentful if he does not get an erection? Do you assume that a man is always capable of sexual arousal? Do you assume responsibility if he is aroused?

2. If you are aware of difficulties in communicating some of your feelings to your partner, you could elicit his views about this chapter.

He is not likely to agree with it all but it can be a useful starting point for discussion between you. Acknowledging and sharing ways in which you both get trapped by the stereotypes is important.

14
Women Loving Women

When we walk down the street, shop on Saturday morning in the supermarket or watch television, we cannot avoid the 'normal' couple. It does not take much to be abnormal. A couple will be 'different' if their ages are very much in contrast, if their skin-colour is very much in contrast or if one or both of them is disabled. Couples will often be aware of this difference in themselves in relation to the social norm. A sexual relationship between two people of the same sex will be equally 'different'. Cultural attitudes towards two men together have tended to exhibit more viciousness and disgust than attitudes towards two women together. This is a direct consequence of the image of women's sexuality in our culture – after all, two passive beings cannot constitute a threat! However, once children are brought into the question, the hostility is awesome. A woman who is sexual in her own right, without a man that is, has to forfeit her right to have children or to look after them or to work with them. The two images, maternal and sexual, cannot be allowed to coexist because this causes a conflict which people cannot tolerate. The only way to release that tension is to hit out.

When it comes to discussing sexual relationships among ourselves, a strong feeling of defensiveness often arises between women who are in sexual relationships with men, and those who are in sexual relationships with women. Discomfort arises from looking at themselves honestly. Heterosexual women can see that their sexual life, their sexual expression is a choice, not a god-given assumption. Pregnancy and childbearing are not their sole prerogative when

139

lesbians are mothers too, which is why lesbian mothers are targets of so much vitriol. Homosexual women are also faced with realizing that their sexual expression is a choice and not necessarily a cause which needs an enemy to exist.

Meeting in a sexuality group provides an opportunity to look at some of these issues and to help open channels of communication between women. This means looking at what is different and what is shared.

Falling in love with a man has one distinct advantage – it is expected of us. Falling in love with a woman means that a woman will become a lot more conscious of what she is doing, simply because it is different. Unless a woman lives in an exclusively lesbian environment, she will be constantly aware of this difference in public. Holding a lover's hand, an impulsive kiss, a friendly squeeze or caress, even sharing an intimate glance are all ordinary tokens of love and affection. But the spontaneity of simple loving gestures is easily inhibited by the felt need to be cautious or openly defiant. A woman who loves other women will have to confront the constant assumption that she is heterosexual, and even if she is not faced with hostility she may well find other people's attitudes frustrating and hurtful. Much of the misunderstanding arises from the stereotypes in our culture.

The mythology about lesbian women reflects the stereotypes discussed in Chapter 3. Pity, ridicule or blame characterize popular attitudes. The stereotyped lesbian has failed in her decorative role as a woman (butch, masculine), she had failed in her functional role as a woman (man-hater, hostile, uncaring, not maternal). She is inadequate or she is invisible. As attention has traditionally been focused on the sexual element between two people, we have a very clear image of the penis and the vagina playing the principal roles in the central drama. Here there is no penis. Since the penis supplies the positive thrust, we are left with two negatives, two minuses which never make a plus. One of the most emphatic notions about female sexuality is that a woman is an empty receptacle waiting for a man to fill her and make her into a real woman. It follows that a sexual relationship between two women will remain fundamentally empty, something always missing, like two empty vessels clattering away in a futile fashion. The idea of two women together rings hollow, not true.

To replace this misleading and negative picture, we can look at the reality of women's own experience. But the answer to the question 'What does it mean to be gay or lesbian or have sexual experiences with other women?' will depend on each individual woman. Her self-definition will vary with her beliefs about herself and her life – the range of experience and beliefs is too varied to specify any general rules.

There are . . .

women who have felt attracted to other women all their lives and have always preferred women as sexual partners;

women who have chosen to relate to women as a political gesture, motivated by a conscious deliberate choice rather than an initial sexual attraction;

women who are happily married, have children and a woman lover as well;

women who have always been attracted to some women and some men;

women who have automatically gravitated to heterosexual marriage before realizing that their sexual preference was for women;

women who feel a strong sexual attraction to just one woman at some time in their lives;

women who love women exclusively and reject men totally as emotional and social companions;

women who love women sexually but don't exclude men as social companions;

women who are turned on to another woman but have never pursued their sexual attraction

. . . too many variations for labels and categories.

Women together

Before looking at some sexual issues among women, it is important to look at this particular partnership in the context of a whole life together. Attention is usually focused on genital activity, but what women do in bed together is secondary to who they are as people together. They share a common oppressive culture, they share a second-class citizenship, they share a low self-esteem, they share bodies and genitals which have been obscured and exploited. They share a knowledge of female rhythms and moods – bleeding, perhaps mothering, being inside a woman's skin. This shared experience can be a bond or a burden, being women together can mean a shared pride or shared resentment. Conditioned as we are to be dependent on men's approval, a relationship with another woman can engender a spirit of rebellion but it can also produce a tension which undermines a relationship if it is not brought out into the open. This tension exists in anyone who goes against the norm. It stems from opposing pressures to conform at every level of our existence – from how we appear, how we behave, how we feel, how we think, who we are sexual with, how sexual we are, how far we get in fulfilling our roles in life.

For some women, sexual relationships with other women have never been a problem. It has always seemed totally natural. But others are faced with areas of concern.

One area is often seen in terms of identity – it can be difficult to establish a positive and celebratory approach to your own feelings and sexual expression in the face of so much negative stereotyping. This may mean being at the receiving end of hostility from strangers or parents; it may mean being patronized by men and women, being dismissed or ignored; the experience of awkwardness at telling other people; or whether to tell them or not. This last will depend on the nature of your secret: a secret which fills you with joy or pride will glow inside you; a secret of which you feel ashamed will fester away, making it difficult for you to feel positive about yourself.

Another complication emerges from the ways in which the myths inhibit us. The myths are pernicious because they have a way of making themselves reality – a gay woman may feel anxious about touching other women for fear they might misunderstand. The myth of the predator can become real enough to inhibit her natural response to reach out in care to touch another human being.

Living an alternative life-style also brings its problems. Although in our heads we can kiss goodbye to tradition, maybe even with a feeling of good riddance, it can sometimes take longer for our hearts to adjust. I have often been surprised that choosing a path which is contrary to the one we are bred for means acknowledging the separation from it, like saying goodbye to part of yourself that will never be. Some women face this when they choose not to have children, others when they realize they never will walk up the aisle in white and be given away. There is often some sadness and grief deep down, which we are afraid to acknowledge because it feels as if we might let the side down! We dismiss our feelings because they are 'irrational' and don't fit in with our *thinking*. Because it doesn't make sense, we often fail to make peace with ourselves at a deep enough level. Making peace, recognizing choice and knowing that choice will mean loneliness at times, enables us to act from a position of strength and self-respect – and also of respect for others.

These are some of the threads of the backcloth against which many sexual relationships between women survive and positively thrive.

Sexual experience between women

It is not surprising that gay women feel reluctant to talk about their sexual experience in view of the cultural exploitation of lesbian lovemaking. In a pornographic context, women make love to one another as a titillation for the on-looking male. There is nothing in it for either of the women – they are there solely to turn on the male and be ready to receive him. A woman can *never* be sexual in her own right. One of the consequences of the way in which women's bodies are turned inside out, objectified and cheapened, is that the celebratory nature of women making love together has been belittled, analysed and mocked time and time again. It is very difficult to hold on to the integrity and understandable that women who love other women express themselves warily or overreact when this is discussed.

Constructing a positive model means finding an option to the current cultural alternatives: either the 'masculine' aggressive approach with its emphasis on seduction and dildos, or the 'feminine' receptive approach, lacking in any thrust and utterly compliant. Whereas the first appears in pornographic films, the second appears more often in ordinary commercial films and films used in sex education or sex therapy which favour affection over lust, passivity over passion, a temperature which is nice and warm but never hot! It seems that women hesitate to make a bold independent statement for fear it may be too strong, but also out of the realistic fear that such a statement would be too confronting and provoke too much hostility.

These stereotypes affect relationships between homosexual and heterosexual women. Some women will 'try it out' with a woman they know to be gay and usually expect her to take the initiative and know what she is doing, thus making the other woman even more vulnerable. Other women gaily assert that they are 'into' women after one sexual nibble at an anonymous breast in a group orgy without realizing how demeaning this kind of illusion is for those women who are in an intimate and committed relationship with another woman and facing all the challenges of such a relationship.

Another way in which this myth is perpetrated is by heterosexual women idealizing woman-to-woman relationships, believing that this will be the answer to their need for love, affection, acceptance and tenderness, but that meanwhile they have to battle on in their relationships with men, almost as if the former were a mere indulgence, again not the *real* thing. In reality, it isn't a bed of roses – just a different bed.

But there is a lot of room for celebration! When women do share their sexual experience with other women, they often find a positive reality. Women enjoy making love with another woman. They enjoy their own rhythms and moods and sensuality with each other. There is a lot of time, touch, tenderness, holding, and skin-talk. Because of the shared experience of being women, they can feel permission to be themselves with their partners. They can let go and trust each other with a passion and fervour which they may have felt was exploited or inhibited in relationships with men.

There is a genuine and natural feeling of equality and friendship. This can occur in heterosexual relationships but it is more difficult, simply because of the culture. It is enormous fun – a lot of play without having to stick to the rules. Women feel more sexually satisfied: 'You can go on and on for ever!' Women describe their experience as very powerful, moving and confronting because there are no roles to hide behind.

Lovemaking can be creative if women construct a rhythm of their own, avoiding measurements or goals. Women can understand more naturally the ups and downs of mood in each other and can recognize the need for lust and thrust at some moments, and tenderness at others. They can understand and feel more affection for a woman's body because they know how it has been abused. A woman can easily love and prize and pleasure every little part of her lover's body without restraint or fear because of a common bond and experience. Cherishing her lover's body is reflected in cherishing her lover as a person in other parts of their lives together.

However, simply being a woman in a relationship with another woman doesn't mean there are never any sexual problems. It is true that the problems may have derived from a male culture but they don't stop simply because a woman stops relating to individual men. There is an often repeated false assumption that making love to another woman is easier because 'it is like making love to yourself' or 'you have the same body so you automatically know what she wants'. First, it implies that a homosexual relationship as immature and narcissistic, rather than acknowledging responsibility towards another human being who is quite separate. Secondly, it simply is not true that we are all the same; women's responses and needs vary greatly. So there can still be problems caused by lack of arousal, insufficient stimulation, the fear of letting go, of difficulty in reaching orgasm. Arousal can still be blocked by emotions, especially anger. Pleasure can still be inhibited by personal messages. Women as lovers are still subject to expectations of sexual behaviour, like needing to have an orgasm to complete a sexual encounter or feeling obliged to take turns rather than appear selfish. Women, as lovers together, are not above the need for clear communication.

Sometimes different norms and rules emerge within lesbian subcultures which still carry overtones of the traditional image. If a woman enjoys something inside her vagina, it is assumed she is dependent on the penis. It is not assumed that she is a woman who enjoys her vagina being stimulated, by fingers or whatever, because the sensation turns her on and gives her pleasure. Sometimes women fear that letting go in orgasm may detract from the equality of the relationship, that one might do something or say something in the heat of the moment that is oppressive. This can reinforce the notion that women's bodies should be controlled at all times and that a woman's sexual excitement should be held in check.

An ideological conflict which emerges every now and then is that a feminist is not a true feminist if she does not relate to women. This makes some women feel guilty if they do not find other women sexually attractive. They may love them, enjoy them as friends, companions, even sensually, but are just not turned on by them. Although the trend in the seventies promoted the idea of natural bisexuality, it is not the reality. Bisexuality came to imply that you were 'into' anyone or anything – men, women, broom-handles, doorknobs – all part of the Superlay image. It became easier to avoid the discomfort of confronting one's true feelings about one's own or the opposite sex. Often this was superficial and 'going both ways' meant a brief encounter with another's genitals rather than an exchange of heart and mind and body and soul.

The fact is that if you are not turned on to someone, then you are not turned on. There are women who feel able to be emotionally and sexually close both to some women and some men. There is often pressure on bisexual women (and men) to come clean and admit their true preference instead of sitting on the fence, but this pressure is usually rooted in the insecurity of each 'side'.

Any true acceptance of another woman's sexual expression, be it on her own or in a relationship with a woman or man, is only possible if we can look at each other from a perspective of being anchored in a sense of personal sexual choice and commitment. Feeling we relate by default or by coercion prevents us accepting that another individual's sexual love is both different *and* the same – not more or less valid.

For the past nine years I have been listening to people's attitudes to all sorts of sexual issues. They haven't changed much and won't until we begin to talk to each other honestly and without the need to convince each other that *one* way is right. Coping with being a woman and one's personal feelings and loves in the face of a hostile society is enough without having to fight norms imposed by other women.

It is tiring to have to justify sexual choices – like many other women I have spent years putting first other people's needs, expectations and wishes, particularly in the area of sexual expression. Women loving women are different in this world and it is a challenge: women loving men in this world also face a challenge. We would do better to talk to each other and listen, learning to be more supportive than divisive. When we believe that our sexuality doesn't depend on a partner, that our bodies belong to ourselves and that we can choose to share this part of ourselves, we can dispense with the need for comparison and competition and start to share a sense of celebration and joy.

15

Breaking the Silence

We find it easy enough to joke about sex. We can talk about it objectively, even knowledgeably. We can understand the words used in titillating descriptions of other people's sexual behaviour recounted in newspapers or books. But when it comes to talking frankly to someone we love about what we are doing together in bed, words mysteriously fail us. Suddenly we can't find the right vocabulary. It all seems absurd or obscene. We feel awkward, tongue-tied and shy.

If you are in a sexual relationship with someone, or have been, you will probably recognize times when you have wanted to ask for more or less of something but, for some reason, you have hesitated. You may also be aware of a recurring pattern when you make love, a pattern that you would like to change but for some reason you can never find the right moment to bring up the subject. Or, if you did, your partner responded with an expression of incomprehension. Perhaps it even led to an argument with the result that you decided it would be much better to leave well alone.

It is not surprising we are inhibited, not surprising that many couples who are able to talk closely about everything else tend to avoid frank and honest dialogue about the sexual aspect of their relationship. We are not helped by the early experience of talking about sex at school or with friends – we usually remember the embarrassment or naughtiness of it, without remembering any information. The very subject has a charge to it and, like money or death, sex is usually considered a delicate topic for discussion. Because this part of our lives evokes such strong feelings, because it feels private and close to the bone, the mere mention of it makes us feel uncomfortable and defensive.

According to society, there are two ways of looking at sex within a relationship. First, it can be romantic. There is a mass of popular literature which conveys that somehow everything just skips into place effortlessly, wordlessly, naturally, magically and simply because two people love one another! It all just *happens*. Or, in contrast, it can be mechanical – an increasing volume of equally popular literature and statistics describes sexual inadequacies and accomplishments based on deeply and widely held assumptions that real sex proceeds in a straight line, starting with arousal (existence of need), moving through certain designated areas of concentrated activity – mouth, breasts, genitals – ending with orgasm (satisfaction of need). Neither model includes the two people actually conversing – silence during sex remains golden!

So if you do want to ask or express something, how are you going to do so without breaking the magic or breaking the routine? The first thing is to give yourself permission to speak and to realize that, like any other area of human interaction, we sometimes need to talk to one another! Such plain common sense contradicts those who vow that they have never 'needed' to talk about it: they got it right first time and haven't looked back since. The arrogance of silence can provide a misty cover for all sorts of real misunderstandings. What you liked ten years ago or even ten minutes ago may have lost its appeal, but how are you or your partner to know this if you are busy pretending that silence automatically conveys satisfaction and success? The most common fear about talking to a sexual partner is that it will suggest you have sexual problems. Fears of inadequacy prevent direct communication and instead you worry about measuring up to the Superlay norm or you worry on your partner's behalf, concerned that they don't quite measure up to some standard of expertise. Although talking does not mean you have problems, not talking will often lead to them. If we don't say what we want to say at the time, it builds up. Tension and resentment accumulate until a major problem does occur – such as switching off completely.

Making requests. Consider first the one-off and relatively small requests which might occur when you make love. There are often many little things we would like to say. Imagine yourself lying there happily making love until you realize your arm has gone to sleep or you need to pee or you feel cold or you find yourself *thinking* about what you are doing, longing to be touched in a different place.

If the cause of your distraction is your personal prude (see Chapter

148

7) then you can use one of the ways suggested to eliminate it and get back into your body and your sensations. But if the cause is related to something actually happening in the present, then you may want to communicate to your partner in some way.

Which of the following describes your characteristic method of communication?

Moving your partner's hand or head or whatever to show where you want more or less action?

A grunt to indicate 'less'?

A wince when a touch is unpleasurable?

A moan to indicate 'more'?

A heavy sigh?

Silent endurance, knowing it won't take long?

Letting your irritation build up and then making a dramatic move?

Speaking up but prefacing what you say with, 'Why don't you ever . . .' or 'How many times do I have to tell you . . .'?

A clear spoken request such as 'I'd love you to squeeze my nipples'?

Those of you familiar with assertiveness training will recognize four basic kinds of communication.

Passive. This way of communicating doesn't actually get anywhere because you do not believe you have a right to ask as you feel that your partner's needs are more important than yours. Sex is someone else's responsibility so you avoid saying anything and just put up with a full bladder or soreness or ambivalence or cold or feeling congested or longing for more stimulation. The person at the receiving end of this kind of communication is often unaware of what is wrong. Over a period of time this can lead to a very unsatisfactory situation, with one partner or both becoming less and less inclined to sexual activity.

Aggressive. After a steady build-up of the passive method of communicating, you let your partner have it, again on the grounds that the responsibility is *theirs*. 'Call yourself experienced?', 'You *have* got a lot of problems, haven't you?' Anxious that one of you might be inadequate, you have to put your partner down to prevent yourself from feeling inferior.

This time, the person on the receiving end will feel quite clearly that *something* is wrong but will not be sure what, and is likely to feel attacked, probably replying in kind.

Indirect. The root of this kind of communication is once again fear of inadequacy – you have to put the other person down, but instead of straight demolition you do it with guilt. You may flinch when you are touched or move a hand away abruptly but never say anything directly. You make it clear that you do not like what is happening, but in such a way as to imply that your partner should have known better! And this is precisely what the person on the receiving end will feel – inadequate, put down, foolish, guilty but without knowing exactly what is wrong.

Assertive. This is clear, specific and direct communication, without blame. The starting point is a feeling of equal responsibility. This is immensely difficult for many women who still secretly believe that they shouldn't have to *say* anything, that if their partners loved them enough, they would know what to do without being told. Failed Sleeping Beauties find it difficult to speak up without a tinge of resentment creeping in!

Equal responsibility starts from a basis of self-knowledge which is one of the crucial factors in successful communication in sexual situations. If you don't know your body you cannot expect someone else to know it for you and if you are going to be clear and specific, you will first of all need to know what it is you do want. The first section of this book has been designed to encourage you to become familiar with what *you* want to make a sexual experience pleasurable: what turns you on and off, awareness of your own body signals, arousal, awareness of your own inhibitions and personal prudes, understanding your limits – all this information makes it possible for you to speak to a partner from a position of responsibility, so you can be both clear and specific and non-critical.

Non-verbal methods, like sounds, are better as an additional rather than the sole means of communication. Although grunts and groans can communicate some things in some situations, their range of expression is limited, whereas a simple word or two is much more effective. And once permission to speak has been established, it is easier to ask if you are not quite sure whether a groan means 'more' or 'stop'.

You don't need to be eloquent – just simple and to the point so you can get on with enjoying yourselves.

That feels amazing.
Down a bit.
Slower.
Up a bit.
I'm a bit sore.
Don't stop.

There!

I'm too tense.

Can you move a bit so I can reach you?

I want another pillow.

I'm cold, can we move the blanket?

I'm losing it.

I'm worried about the time.

I want to stop a minute.

That's wonderful.

Oh yes.

Asking for information. This doesn't have to be a personal interrogation but there are often times when you would like to know whether what you are doing is what your partner wants. This concern, like any thought or anxiety, will interfere with your own arousal – and there is nothing worse than going through the motions of 'pleasuring' someone when your heart and body aren't in it. We hesitate in fear of being judged as ignorant or inadequate lovers. But it can be frustrating and when it reaches a high point, we lash out and put down the other person. '*How* long did you say you took to come?' If your partner's response is unclear, and you are not sure if you are reading the signals correctly, you may want to check it out. If you want to know where to touch, how hard to go, where to stimulate, exactly what your lover would really like, you can give yourself permission to ask.

Do you want to try something else?

Do you want me to go harder?

Do you want me to stop?

How is it just there?

As you can see, you are not asking your partner to keep up a running commentary – just wanting to make sure you are giving pleasure so that you clear your own doubts and allow yourself to be absorbed in the pleasure of pleasuring!

Saying no. Most of us make a hash of saying no clearly at the best of times, and in a sexual situation we tend to be at our worst. Our difficulties arise from a variety of factors: feeling responsible for someone else's arousal; being habitually unclear about our own needs; failing to recognize our own bodies' signals because we are more concerned with the other person; and finally a lack of skill in making an assertive refusal. This means a refusal which is clear, direct, non-aggressive but firm.

You may have found yourself wanting to say no to starting a sexual relationship. Have you ever wanted to refuse a social invitation which you felt would end up with a sexual invitation? Or to refuse to get involved further in a sexual relationship? Or wanted to act on a mutual attraction to someone?

Knowing yourself means you have a clear indication of what you want. Do you want to start a sexual relationship, and, if so, what are the limits? Are you attracted to this person? If not, then why are you even considering going ahead with sexual activity? If you are, then do you actually want to be sexual? Are the circumstances right for you and the other person? Have you considered other commitments? Does it make sense? If it does, then you are able to negotiate; if not, you will need to say no. This whole area is so fraught that messing around with vague half-truths and politeness is unfair to yourself and the other person. You can still be friendly in your refusal: 'I'm attracted to you but (for whatever reason) I do not want to be sexual with you' or 'I like you/respect you/enjoy your company, but I do not want to go to bed with you.'

Why are we frightened of saying no clearly? It can be because we anticipate loss of approval. This fear stems from a low self-esteem. If we feel our sexual identity depends on someone finding us attractive, then we are going to find it a lot more difficult to say no. We fear rejection or loneliness or that no one will ever ask us again. Or we fear verbal aggression – being put down or belittled or perhaps being physically harassed or assaulted.

Taking a firm stand at the outset can prevent the build-up of non-verbal pressure. The longer we leave it, the worse it gets. We often endure the hands, the grope, the unwanted proximity because of a rising uncertainty: 'Is he doing what I think he's doing or is it my imagination?' As the pressure increases, so does our level of anxiety, making it even more difficult to be clear. We can save ourselves a lot of unnecessary tension and aggravation by being clear at the beginning.

There may still be embarrassment, of course. In this culture, it is just not expected that a woman will be direct: she is expected to play the game. But games can hurt all the people concerned and even if there is a little temporary awkwardness in the air, she can feel confident that she has been honest and that she acted with the right intention. In the long run it will pay off. Sometimes, women get quite entangled in a relationship, agreeing to social and even long drawn out sexual encounters when they would have liked to say no at the start. Extrication halfway through is much worse than setting limits in the first place.

Saying no in an on-going relationship isn't any easier. All of us have times when we don't feel in the mood because we feel physically low or tired or preoccupied or angry or something just isn't right. The difficulty in saying no to a long-term partner is rooted in the same insecurity and fear of losing approval. We find it difficult to give ourselves *permission* to feel non-sexual. If you are married, you may believe, as your husband does, that it is your duty. After all, much of our social and religious heritage has persuaded husbands that their wives are there to obey them in everything, and such things take an awful long time to change. Perhaps you believe a man's need is urgent and more desperate. Or you may fear a grumpy response or getting involved in an argument or being criticized and put down or attacked. Many women fear that their husbands will go elsewhere for satisfaction – echoes of the beast on the rampage again. The truth is that men can take no for an answer.

We can all accept a refusal if it is given clearly and with care. A clear and caring refusal is something you may not have learned how to do as a woman – I certainly didn't. I was taught that if I cared, I had to say yes – I couldn't believe that I could love someone and say no at the same time. But, of course, sometimes we do need to say no to those we love. Usually guilt and anxiety and lack of practice will interfere with clarity so we often say no passively or aggressively or indirectly instead.

A passive 'no'. This means accommodating the other person, going along with it, putting nothing in and getting nothing out. Gradually, you can turn yourself off, numbing your body to sexual response because you are going against your body's own wisdom.

An aggressive no. This basically consists of blaming the other person for asking, with comments like: 'How dare you?', 'Stop pawing me', 'Haven't you grown out of it yet?', 'You must be oversexed. You should see a doctor!' Any remark or gesture which uses attack to block someone else's wishes is aggressive.

An indirect no. This includes excuses like the proverbial 'headache'. An indirect refusal is similar to the aggressive but more subtle. 'How can you ask me that when you know I'm tired?' 'I thought you would show more sensitivity!' This includes going to bed early to avoid sex or staying up late and waiting till you hear your partner's snores; or starting a row early on in the evening to ensure you won't be speaking to each other when it comes to bedtime!

Any of the above methods will make the point eventually, but if you want to give your partner the double message – that you care *and* you are saying 'no' – then an assertive refusal is more effective.

An assertive 'no'. This may mean an outright no: 'I'm sorry, but I'm just not in the mood', 'I want to be close but I really don't want to make love.' A frequent objection to being assertive is the wish to keep our options open. Some women say that even if they start off reluctantly they can soon get into the swing of it and ultimately enjoy themselves. The problem is that this is exactly what leads to the myth that when a woman says no, she really means yes. It is important, if you are uncertain, to say so: that way you keep your options truly open. You may begin to get aroused and want to go on, or continue to be only slightly aroused and want to stop. If you want to compromise, you can negotiate – a little action but not the full works. Failing to set limits in advance can lead to resentment and disappointment. If you are prepared to negotiate openly, you can be responsible for yourself and also fair to your partner. This kind of communication is inevitably difficult because it goes against the norm of not actually saying anything. But silence carries the risk of misunderstanding, hurt, unhappiness and frustration when a few simple, caring words at the right time can make all the difference.

It will certainly build up a climate of trust and permission between you. It also helps when you want to consider tackling bigger issues in your sexual relationship. Apart from one-off situations, there may be a general pattern which has developed over the time you have been together. This makes it more difficult to handle because, instead of dealing with something when it was small and manageable, you may have let your dissatisfaction or irritation build up over two months or two years or twenty years!

Your own pattern of sexual activity with your partner will be unique but you may recognize one or more of the following elements. One factor is lack of arousal which usually means that the conditions you need to feel sexually aroused are not being met. There may be something you can do about this on your own but you may also need your partner's cooperation.

Examples of complaints that women might make are:

a) We always do it at night when I'm tired.
b) He doesn't touch me very much beforehand.
c) I wish it weren't always so predictable.

The very first rule in changing a sexual pattern with a partner is to identify a clear request. What is it you want to be different? Making a complaint or issuing a demand that your lover be more sensitive is avoiding taking responsibility for your own needs and is unhelpful in terms of communication. The above examples might be phrased along these lines:

a) I feel too tired to make love at night. Can we try at some other time like in the morning or weekends?
b) I feel distant and unaroused when we go straight into sex without touching. I would like to spend more time relaxing and being close beforehand.
c) I would like to experiment a little. What do you think?

The exact words don't matter as much as the fact that you are making a clear request. Then at least your partner will know what you want, before deciding whether or not to cooperate.

Another factor is differing likes and dislikes or different rhythms and needs.

a) My lover wants to make love more often than I do.
b) I don't like oral sex but my partner does.
c) I don't want to have intercourse every time we make love.

Again you need to be specific about what you want before discussing it with your partner, then you can negotiate fairly.

a) You could check out your partner's feelings about the frequency of sexual activity. Often we punish ourselves with the Superlay myth when in reality it is unnecessary. Or you can compromise: you may be willing to have some sexual contact but want to set limits at the same time.
b) Are you uncomfortable with receiving it? If so, is this how it is done or your own discomfort with your genitals? Or you may feel unhappy about pleasuring your partner in this way. If your partner is a man maybe you do not like him coming in your mouth – in which case, again, you can ask for some limits.
c) And if you want to make love without always having intercourse, then you could suggest an alternative.

The important rule is to take responsibility for yourself. But because the situation is sensitive, it can help to remember some useful guidelines which build a climate of cooperation and trust.

Choose your time and place wisely. This means never just before, during or after sexual activity. We are all far too vulnerable at such times to be able to listen to criticism. And women as well as men suffer from performance anxiety. None of us like to be told we are incompetent and since our defences are down when we are sexually aroused, a criticism, however beautifully phrased or well-intentioned, hits right below the belt. Arrange a time in advance away from chores and other responsibilities; have a meal together or go for a walk. The essential point is to be alone with some time in hand.

Take joint responsibility. It is tempting to get mileage out of blaming your partner, but the only way you will ever get anyone to listen is by acknowledging that it takes two. You may need to accept criticism yourself. This may also mean asking for some suggestions in return as to how you could change your behaviour. It is because we often don't want to hear criticism about ourselves that we don't bring up the subject in the first place, although our official reason usually is that we don't want to hurt the *other* person.

Remember the power of the cultural mythology and tread carefully. It is dangerous to want to turn our partners into the fantasy lovers which our culture has deeply conditioned us to expect. The myth of Superlover/Superlay has had a pernicious effect on our ability to be sexually open with each other. Intimacy includes seeing the other person as they are, and accepting them as you accept yourself. The less you pressure yourself, the less pressure you will need to exert on a partner. And, conversely, the more you accept yourself as an independent sexual being, the more you will be able to honour your own needs.

Watch for unrealistic expectations. If a breakdown in sexual communication is only the tip of the iceberg, no amount of clear requests will make any difference. There is little point in asking your husband to touch your breasts more often if you hate him so much that what you really want is a divorce! Nor is it going to work if your need for more affection reflects a much deeper need for affection that you didn't get from one of your parents: no adult can ever replace what we miss out on as children. It is equally unrealistic to expect an enjoyable sexual interaction when either you or your partner are under some kind of severe stress. No amount of effort will overcome ordinary human limitations.

The meanings of sex

Another complication is that people have sex for all sorts of reasons.

Having a fuck or making love isn't as simple as it sounds when the sharing of physical sex can acquire a different meaning at different times within different relationships. These are just a few examples.

Physical need. Sexual activity is enjoyed because one or both people feel a sexual desire which leads to the need for satisfaction.

Making up. Sex can be a way of resolving an argument, smoothing the prickles, a way to cut through the residual tension and touch base together again.

Getting even. Withdrawing or conceding, sex becomes a channel for resentment, a context in which to make one's point effectively when the other person is needy and vulnerable.

Closeness. Sexual contact can become the only time when a person is touched, so the drive towards sex represents the opportunity to be held, loved and given some attention.

Avoiding intimacy. It is sometimes easier to launch into the old routine rather than take the risk of talking to each other. Sex can become a diversion from the more confronting intimacy of sharing angry or hurt feelings with a partner.

Relieving tension. Sex can be a distraction, a way of forgetting everything else, temporarily putting aside all the hassles and just enjoying the release of emotional and physical tension.

Reinforcement. Sex can be used as a reinforcement of power within a relationship or establishing dependency. It comes to symbolize the basic emotional patterns which keep the two people together.

Booster. In a life of over-commitment and responsibility, sex also provides an opportunity for *time* with a partner, as a way of renewing contact and love.

You may be aware of many other variations. The point is that the complexity can make it difficult to steer a clear course through this emotional minefield. This is why I would recommend acquiring assertive skills in other less charged situations before tackling sexual difficulties in an intimate relationship. Practice in role-play beforehand can often reveal hidden agendas between you and your partner, which will get in the way if unacknowledged.

This is why it is so much better to start at the beginning and learn to communicate simple one-off requests as described earlier in this chapter. Doing this helps you feel more in charge and can be very positive and powerful. This is how one woman described her own experience: 'The other night, G wanted to fuck and I didn't. I needed loving. Before the course, I could have given the no with a "headache", self-righteous indignation or a put-down. I would have seen him *needing* me and thought guiltily, well, it wouldn't take long;

I would have found it nigh on impossible to voice what my own need was without putting myself down. During and through the course, I began the long process of reclaiming my body. At last I felt that I knew it. I believed that I owned it. I felt certain of my right to say no and was gradually able to know and ask for what I needed and to feel okay about that for the very first time!'

Go gently. Even if you do identify a specific need and ask without aggression, as this woman did, you are still dependent on a third factor: the willingness of your partner to listen. It may take time for your partner to understand. Whether your partner is a man or a woman, it could be a gradual process for him or her to trust you enough to admit to not knowing your body too precisely, to be able to ask you for something directly, to be able to express a difficulty or inhibition. Another difficulty arises when you are asked the question, 'Why haven't you said anything *before*?' This is one of the strongest inhibitions for many of us – how can we make a fresh start after colluding for so long? It can be handled with honesty and joint responsibility but it does take time and care.

No matter how assertive you are, if you have a partner who refuses to cooperate, there is little you can do but acknowledge there is a difference between persistence and useless perseverance. Similarly, your partner may want to cooperate but, no matter what, they are unable to change. You may well feel that because you love the person so much in every other way, it doesn't matter and sex can become a less important part of your relationship or you may decide that sexual pleasure is important to you. Only you can decide what your limits are in this situation.

We are all so vulnerable and we face such a huge cultural barrier that it will take time just to get used to the idea of *talking* about sex. But the rewards are there. Breaking the barrier of silence the first time is the worst and after that it gets easier. And by the means of simple, clear, on the spot communication, you can avoid the emotional backpile and enjoy more pleasure, more directness and more equality.

Apart from the normal ups and downs which effect sexual feelings, there are three particular times when many women experience unhappiness and stress. These are three times of transition – to womanhood, to motherhood and to middle age. Each stage is heralded by bodily changes due to the activities of hormones – at the onset of menstruation, during pregnancy and childbirth and with the menopause. So research has tended to concentrate on the hormonal aspect in an attempt to control unwanted symptoms with hormonal adjustments. But we know that it is not only what happens inside her body which affects a woman but what it means to her. How will this change reduce or enhance her femininity, her external prestige, her social value? Her conflicts and concerns about these changes can precipitate a time of transition into a time of crisis. Although some women pass through different stages in their lives without noticing very much at all, many experience being a teenager, or becoming a mother, or entering middle and old age as a time of confusion, moodiness, anxiety, depression, or despair.

Whenever we are subject to change in our lives, we are vulnerable: for example, moving house, redundancy, retirement, a new relationship, a new job, divorce, a death in the family, each in their own way presents a time of transition. We need to say goodbye to one thing and greet something new. Until we have truly adjusted to the new stage we are more emotionally vulnerable than at other times, and periods of transition in our sexual lifecycle are no exception.

Because of this, we are more susceptible to all sorts of feelings which lie dormant most of the time. Our defences are down because of our physical changes and suddenly these feelings rise to the surface. The difficulty is that neither we nor those around us understand what is happening or why we are so 'upset'. Measures considered appropriate are taken to help us through a bad time but rarely do we use this experience to learn from our feelings. We can feel crazy and alone, often not realizing that the source lies not within ourselves but in the conflict *between* ourselves and the environment in which we live. With more understanding of this interplay, we can approach any transition with less fear and self-blame and more acceptance and support.

Sexuality and adolescence

With the onset of menstruation, a young woman has to leave childhood behind her. She learns through menstruation that her genitals are part of her reproductive equipment and that each month her body prepares for the possibility of motherhood. An internal process is affecting her body in ways she cannot control. She turns her attention towards external appearance. This she feels more able to control. She may be eager to abandon girlhood and to 'grow up' – she may prefer the security of being a child. Conflict sometimes emerges in excessive dieting or compulsive eating, which offer some measure of control over her changing, developing body.

As a daughter, a girl learns the need to be attractive and win a husband. She learns to accentuate and capitalize on certain parts of her body. In cultural terms, she is at the peak of her decorative potential. She learns that sexuality equals sex equals sexual activity and that she had better be careful not to get pregnant because she will lower her price on the heterosexual market. Even if she does receive the bare bones of sex education, she will learn little of emotions, relationships and, least of all, of the importance of an attitude of pride, joy and knowledge of her own body. This will be superseded by the need to appear attractive to others, as long as she exercises caution and restraint. She is likely to experiment sexually to gain status, but has little concern for her own pleasure.

One of the reasons that the cultural messages are so powerful at this time is that a young woman in her teens can feel pulled towards establishing external sexual status as one way of coping with the conflict she feels with her parents. The messages at home about female sexuality are ambiguous. A daughter's blossoming sexual development can awaken all sorts of memories in her mother, which bring back unexpressed feelings. The beginning in her daughter may be an unwelcome reminder of her own decline. The young woman may look at her mother competitively, see her getting older, pity her or blame her for not being more positive. Many women who remember this time as a time of unhappiness recall a longing to be able to talk to their mothers, a desire for closeness and reassurance which never came. The most difficult problem is not the emerging feelings but the lack of communication between mother and daughter at this particular time.

This is further compounded by the change in the relationship between daughter and father. His love for her also faces a crisis. His awareness of his daughter as a sexual being can make him uneasy. Now that she is no longer a child, he fears his own responses, the ever-lurking monster within. Since he rarely talks to anyone, the internal conflict can be too much to bear. And as a man, he generally reacts to fear with aggression or avoidance. Some fathers aggressively override the vulnerability of the young girl so as not to feel their own. The experience of sexual abuse or incest, whether with her father or other male relatives, will distort her perception of herself even further. And this experience is far more widespread than we like to admit.

Avoidance, on the other hand, leads to withdrawal. The father may find it safer to avoid all contact. If this happens, his daughter often feels rejected as his affection and interest are withdrawn and many bitter arguments ensue as the father's conflict finds expression in excessive punishment or criticism. In adolescence, she looks at her body with a new awareness and ambivalence: she knows that her sexuality is the cause of her rejection but at the same time she realizes her power.

Separating from her father emotionally is helped by finding an adult male sexual relationship, although some women never manage to let go the need for a male partner to be a father-figure. However, separation from her mother is more difficult. There is too much left unsaid between them, too much unresolved, easier to run away from than confront and talk through with each other.

Sexuality and motherhood

Culturally, a woman is now at her functional peak. Her body has undergone a period of acquiescence – it has been taken over not only by the growth of a being inside her but also by the medical profession. Her sexual and bodily feelings will be affected by the physical experience of pregnancy and childbirth, a process over which she exerts little control. It is often after birth, particularly after a first baby, that a woman is emotionally very open to confusion and depression. Much of this relates to her changing view of her body, her self and her sexuality. The transition is felt from being 'one' with the child to seeing the child as having a separate existence *outside* her body. The two of them are no longer a unit. The baby often appears a stranger at first and it can take time to accept and love this tiny individual. The transition from woman to mother strikes a profound sense of responsibility. She is no longer free to do what she could before. At first she can often feel she is acting a part that doesn't seem real to her.

Coping with the demands of a new routine add to the intense fatigue experienced after birth. When the mother is home and taking responsibility for the baby, its demands will be exhausting. There is also the cumulative effect of lack of sleep so that it is difficult to avoid feeling utterly shattered and quite unable to cope with the simple tasks of everyday existence. Fatigue will enhance *her* need to be mothered. The new responsibility and feeling out of step with her body will mean she herself needs to be cosseted. Friends and partners and grandparents give lots of attention to the baby, but a new mother can long for closeness.

Any thought or discussion of sexuality at this time will be confined to sexual activity. She may find that with all these other changes, she has become less interested in intercourse and more in need of a gentle approach. She may be unwilling to take the initiative. Some of this is due to the effects of being manhandled in hospital. When her body has been critically assessed and impersonally examined as an object it is difficult to open up and trust herself to receive pleasure. The after-effects of obstetric surgery increase sensitivity. Until her hormones get back to normal, her vagina may not lubricate: she may still feel pain or *fear* pain and there may be unhappy memories surrounding labour and birth. All of this will affect her ability to enjoy her body sexually, to become aroused, and to trust her partner.

Unfortunately, women's own lack of assertiveness and men's lack of sexual options mean that misunderstandings often occur and can continue for years afterwards just because of lack of consideration at the time.

Another difficulty in her adult sexual relationship is that, for the first time, she catches a glimpse of another aspect of sexuality.

Because of the lack of intimacy between many men and women as adults, a new mother can become absorbed in a love affair with her infant. She may feel that the baby makes her body complete, like a missing part replaced. It is something, maybe the only thing which *belongs* to her. So much of our learned behaviour and expectations get in the way of male-female relationships and sexual interaction, that a mother, faced with a tiny child, can find an intensity and eroticism in their interaction which is missing from her sexual activity with her partner. Kissing, stroking, nuzzling, many spontaneous exchanges of affection become totally absorbing and are marked by a total lack of self-consciousness. Pleasure with this being is permitted without judgement or the restrictive need for approval. She may find it embarrassing to talk about and be worried about excluding her partner. Even though this lack of inhibition and intimacy changes as a child grows up, many women continue to enjoy a closeness with their children which is unparalleled in their adult relationships. Presumably this is why many women are able to go without sexual affection and not seek affairs – they are content without genital sex because of the fulfilment of this particular intimacy with their children.

When a woman sees her body for the first time after birth she can find it a traumatic experience. She can be upset by the bundles of flesh, the folds, the flabbiness. But some women feel a sense of relief – their functional role has taken over. They don't feel they have to keep up with a media image because having a child, being a mother, releases them from this need. They don't see the need to be decorative because they don't see themselves as sexual. Somehow motherhood and sexuality don't seem to fit! Breastfeeding can be sexually stimulating and a highly erotic experience which is suppressed in many women who feel they shouldn't be getting turned on by such a motherly activity! The culture would certainly have us believe that sexual and maternal feelings do not go together at all. One way in which maternal and sexual are seen as incompatible is the change in public perception of our breasts. The very same breasts which are acceptable in the newsagent's, serving drinks or exposed in films are suddenly considered something dirty, something which should be hidden away from public view. A woman's breasts in a decorative context are prized – in a functional context, they become offensive!

Similarly, a woman can feel that maternal emotions are not compatible with sexual emotions. Some women express an inhibition about making love while a child is anywhere in the house or feel uneasy about talking about sex or acknowledging sexual feelings. They have a deep sense that it is not fitting for a *mother*. And this affects the expression of anger as well. Love is considered as the maternal emotion and anger is associated with the assertive and the sexual. Sexual needs and desires are not compatible with the receptive, nurturing, passive role expected of her so these two emotions of love and anger make uncomfortable bedfellows. This incompatibility can extend as long as a mother continues her role, and it is very difficult for many women to express their natural frustration and anger to their children and to their partners when such displays of feeling evoke public disapproval.

Sexuality and middle age

Menopause describes a series of bodily symptoms which can occur over a period of several months or years, but whether a woman experiences menopause at forty or fifty, there is likely to be a time when emotionally she has to come to terms with the meaning of her changing body. Although she will have to make further physical and emotional adjustments as she enters old age and faces the prospect of her death, the menopause has a particular significance in this culture.

In a way similar to adolescence, she looks at her body with a new awareness. Much of what happens in middle age refers to the loss of physical attractiveness. Losing one's figure, losing one's looks, getting lines and wrinkles, developing a spare tyre, thickening ankles are all comments one associates with middle and old age. If a woman's self-esteem has depended heavily on being judged attractive, she will probably face a crisis. With the widespread emphasis on youth, she will have been aware for some time of a decline in her decorative value. She may want to avoid or disguise the physical changes and preserve a youthful image. She may feel worried that she will lose her viability as a sexual woman. Since sexuality is still seen as a sexual activity, viability means her ability to turn her partner on. This can be difficult when men of the same age are often tempted to prop up their own floundering sense of morale by aiming their sights at younger, attractive women.

The majority of women will face some kind of sexual readjustment. With hormonal changes, the vagina will not be so easily lubricated and although this can be helped with a substitute, some women may feel uncomfortable using one. Quite often, it is not only the physical changes which affect sexual activity but the personal prude which whispers that sexual needs are unseemly after a certain age! A woman's sexual arousal and enjoyment can be positively affected by the menopause. When menstruation stops many women are delighted, particularly if periods have been painful and regarded a nuisance and also because they can enjoy sex without fear of pregnancy.

For others, the loss of menstruation can constitute a crisis: if a woman's self-esteem has depended heavily on her nurturing role in the past, this aspect will probably cause her most difficulty. With the need to be needed, she will find it hard to face her dependents leaving home and find it difficult to stand up on her own. She may take in an ageing parent or look to outside voluntary work to continue this role.

At this time, women can look forward to a new lease of life. Without children as a glue, they may look at their partners and their relationships in a different light – this can be a chance for a new beginning, together or alone. Many feel held back by their own fear: fear of freedom, fear of success, fear of their own capabilities. And picking up a working life after all this time with all the attendant disadvantages of lack of training and experience can be a severe test of confidence. Some women do put this surge of energy and independence to positive use. However, some women report that their husbands are disconcerted by these bold new ventures and satisfactions *outside* the home and they find themselves actively discouraged and unsupported at this important time.

The 'change' can be a mixed blessing. Transition will take time. After a busy life at home, devoted to bringing up a family, many women find themselves confronted with a silence which is awesome. And a woman who has not had children may find herself on the receiving end of unwelcome pity from other women who cannot imagine what on earth a woman can look forward to in her later years without grandchildren.

Many women find that after the crisis of menopause, this time in their lives is very positive. Theirs is a shared richness, a sense of having weathered many storms and survived. No doubt this helps to combat the persistent putdowns from medical personnel and the patronage of younger professionals who share the assumption that middle-aged women are stupid or past it: if *all* a woman has done is to have been a housewife and mother, she is considered to have no resources or intelligence at all! Because of our culture, it is not surprising that many middle-aged women feel from time to time that they have been put on society's scrap heap – a feeling which (for men too), increases with the years.

In any society, rites of passage are marked in a way which embodies that society's attitudes to the female life process. In our own, these three phrases can be roughly characterized as potential, fulfilment and decline. The result is that many young girls are not encouraged to explore their potential in any area other than marriage, that women often have children without really considering the repercussions and the responsibility, and that women in middle and old age are a completely overlooked resource of experience and wisdom. As our sexuality has become so distorted, we lose the opportunity to get to know ourselves a little more, we lose out on occasions for marking, for mourning and for welcoming and celebrating the new. Instead, each change reflects our objective cultural value with the following consequences.

The result for many women is a continuing **circle of dependence**. A daughter doesn't ever really detach herself from her mother, and transfers her dependence from mother to husband. She may then become a mother herself and learn to be depended upon. Later in life, she may in turn become dependent on her children. This circle of dependency means that many women find it difficult to relate as an equal adult but can only understand relationships either as being dependent on another or having another dependent on themselves. With a choice of helpless child or responsible mother, women are often unable to consider equality and independence.

The second result is a continuous theme of **denial**. There is very little direct communication between daughter and mother at the onset of menstruation, and about sexual behaviour in adolescence. If she feels unhappy about her situation, she will learn to deny and not complain. Protest seems pointless. When she is a mother herself for the first time, she may well find her mother still unable to communicate. She learns to deny the pain she experiences as a conspiracy of silence transmits the denial from mother to daughter, from woman to woman. Many women want to talk to their own mothers about their experience, to have confirmation and reassurance, but find their mothers unable to understand why they should want to dredge up all those things from the past. Since motherhood is considered the natural and inevitable function of a woman, she is expected to assume this function with acceptance and not complain or express anger at her situation. Anger and resentment are withheld, like the expression of pain, because they are not compatible with the public image of a loving and capable mother. The physical pain of labour and delivery is denied by a desire not to be a nuisance to the hospital staff, and so women offer their bodies uncomplainingly and passively for treatment. Their helplessness in this context is symptomatic of a much wider sense of helplessness. Realizing the extent of this powerlessness is sometimes too difficult for women to acknowledge, even to themselves. Women don't want to appear ungrateful or unbalanced and so they insist that everything is all right, rather than face the truth. Denial of pain and denial of helplessness risk denial of pleasure and denial of power. Once we can admit to one, we can acknowledge the other!

The third theme is **comparison.** From a position of apparent powerlessness we fight even harder to earn some little validity and recognition. We compare our status and look to each other from a shared base of low self-esteem. A mother can feel jealous of her blossoming teenage daughter. Those with children feel superior to those who are without. The older woman feels that it is too late for her to change. The younger woman feels she's got more going for her than the older woman. The mistress wants to provide what the unfortunate wife cannot.

All of this revolves around a woman's sexuality being her main resource in the present economic system. Most women do not have any real choice about whether or not to follow this designated path. In poorer countries, women have no hope of financial survival outside the security of the family structure, and even in wealthier countries, opportunities for women to seek achievement in other spheres are open only to a tiny minority. Our dependency makes us more and more vulnerable and helpless. Our sexuality no longer belongs to us.

Imagine how different it would be if a woman believed her sexuality and her body were her own. The concept of sexuality in a matriarchal culture offered a view of what it could be like. Instead of the three roles of daughter, mother, grandmother, as defined by this culture, the three faces of a woman's sexuality were represented by the images of virgin, mother and crone. The virgin was a woman of *any* age who was sexually active but had no children and no permanent partner. She belonged to herself. Sexuality was believed to be a continuous state of being rather than confined to those periods when a woman was in a sexual relationship. When a woman chose to have children she didn't lose her sexuality. She remained a person. Motherhood and nurturing didn't mean loss of self. And before the word was trivialized, crone meant a wise woman who didn't lose her beauty and her body and was a source of spiritual wisdom as she approached the end of her physical life.

Instead of dependence, imagine a sense of autonomy, a belief in a fundamental beauty which started inside and spread outwards. No dependence, no comparison. Imagine female sexuality *celebrated* as an interweaving process – very much in tune with the rhythms and cycles of nature, with no phase less or more important than the other but each part of a cycle. Changing faces of an integrated, earthly and spiritual power.

How can we use these transitions positively today? The answer lies in seeing our changing sexuality as a cycle rather than a diminishing line; a cycle in which our sexual energy, sexual interest, sexual expression, sexual activity, ebb and flow; a small-scale cycle which is reflected within each month and a larger-scale cycle which is reflected in the changes and rhythms of our bodies through the years. Viewed in this way, we could more easily accept the process of life and death and we could see that each stage mirrors the others. A sense of connection would help us to be much more supportive and, more important, we could *talk* to each other. We cannot do a lot to change the status quo all at once, but we can stop pretending that everything is fine or expressing total resignation to fate.

If mothers talked directly to their daughters much conflict would be avoided. Menstruation could be positively recognized as an important transition and one worthy of celebration, giving a daughter a gesture of positive encouragement to help her stand firm in the face of the negative response she will inevitably encounter. Practical sex education could include information about masturbation and, especially, skills in assertive refusal. She could be encouraged to value her body as something special.

A young mother will need time for herself. Her transition calls for sensitivity and care from those around her. Recognizing that she may need personal cosseting at this time can help. If her partner is a man, he could be less insistent and concerned with intercourse than with other ways of enjoying sex together. Assertive communication helps all round.

She will need acceptance of her anger should it emerge. She may feel the strain of trying to be the perfect mother and need to talk about it. Fortunately, the pioneering work in changing attitudes towards women and childbirth has resulted in groups for mothers when they leave hospital which can provide a much-needed opportunity to talk through feelings and anxieties in a supportive environment. She may want to affirm the pain she experienced. This doesn't mean wittering on endlessly about it but simply acknowledging it despite having been told that she will soon forget. Many women don't want to forget the pain. Even if childbirth has been the most intensely painful experience their bodies have been through, the pain *and* the pleasure of giving birth were equally important aspects of the whole experience.

The positive side of ageing is coming to terms with new horizons and a different body. Adjustment is not the same as restriction. Going alone or with a friend to have a sauna or massage or steam bath, any pleasurable experience is a great way to contradict the feeling of being put on the scrap heap. We can give up the idea that we are too old to change and have to apologize for increasing years. It's difficult of course in a culture which tells us differently, but we can stop trying to hide our ageing relatives, suggesting discreetly that they cover up their wrinkles or should not be having sex or even thinking about it. Instead of living in isolation, many women are finding that it is proving emotionally and economically preferable to set up home with each other when, for whatever reason, they find themselves without a partner in middle and old age.

Breaking the conspiracy of silence is the most effective way of counteracting the invisibility of female sexuality. I am often inspired by the story of one woman who was so struck by the experience of self-examination in class that she recounted to her mother what they had done. One question led to another and eventually they agreed to try it out together. Although full of trepidation, she found it a wonderful and moving experience to look at her mother's genitals, to see where she had 'come from' and to acknowledge so simply and directly a *shared* womanhood and sexuality between daughter and mother. And if you find yourself reacting with horror to the idea of doing this with *your* mother, you will understand exactly what this chapter is about!

17

Women as Friends

If two people today are seen to be enjoying each other's company, sharing warmth and affection, making the time to be with each other, sooner or later someone is likely to wonder 'What is going on?' From adolescence onwards, friendships are tolerated as a phase but it is clear that an individual is encouraged and expected to move on to heterosexual coupling and fulfilment. Throughout our lives, the predominant model of significant adult relationships is one in which sexual activity has been or still is an intrinsic part. Consequently, we are familiar with celebrating the occasion of a first or seventieth anniversary of a marriage but, as I found when celebrating twenty years of a particular friendship recently, there is little public acknowledgement of the importance and value of friendship. Friendship between women, between men and between women and men suffers a general devaluation in a heterosexually obsessed culture. Friendship between women is trivialized as just a gossip and a giggle, an exchange of the inanities which fill female heads and lives. Friendship between women and men also suffers from cultural restrictions and expectations.

Women as friends with men

Friendship between the opposite sexes poses problems. This applies to the friendship within a sexual and intimate relationship as well as to a completely non-sexual relationship. Either way, the notion of friendship can suffer from a fundamental lack of equality. A friend is someone with whom you feel essentially equal so the cultural disparity between men and women makes it difficult for them to be close friends. Stepping out of the sexual roles makes friendship possible, but this also entails discarding the defence of stereotyped and predictable behaviour. From a man's point of view, this can be a further drawback because it means he will have to confront his difficulty in being emotionally close and will find himself treading through unchartered territory. Friendship does not have the 'safe' demarcation of sexual interaction: it involves vulnerability.

Many women find friendship with men difficult because they find that unless sex is *somewhere* on the agenda, however remote a possibility, many men aren't interested. They do not consider it worth the effort to put energy and time and thought into what will turn out to be a waste of time. The challenge is missing, the thrill of the chase is absent so they do not believe there is any point in bothering. It is too frightening to risk interaction with women without a clearly defined goal.

This works both ways. Women too are sometimes secretly keeping an eye out for the possibility of sex. Whether he is heterosexual or homosexual, women still look out for a sign that they are seen as sexual beings. A woman may find it difficult to accept the fact that she is not sexually attractive to a particular man, especially if she likes him. It doesn't necessarily mean that she wants to act on it, indeed she is ready to refuse, but it's reassuring just to be asked!

People don't go to singles bars for friendship. This is where sex really does rear its ugly head. We are so accustomed to believing that sex has to be a part of any worthwhile relationship, we can feel pressurized to include it somewhere. Or to feel that there is something missing if 'it' doesn't happen. Sex always seems to be hovering in the background and so we are encouraged not to give up hope entirely. A positive model for non-sexual friendship between men and women is clearly lacking.

Another obstacle is the changing attitudes of the times. Any kind of relationship between a man and a woman will come up against the notion of sexism in some way. This can be avoided more easily with the existence of sexual attraction: enjoying yourself in bed makes it seem that what is happening in the world out there has nothing to do with you and *your* man. But with no sexual activity and no intention of getting there, we face each other more nakedly than in bed, as the nature of our roles in the culture is changing. Because of defensiveness about feminism it is easy to tread on each other's toes, or to avoid the issue altogether. But, like anything which we avoid, it continues to lurk in the background. Men are encouraged by the media and by some individual women to believe that what women want is to turn the tables, to seek revenge and make men suffer for what has happened. This is a lamentably short-sighted, though popular, attitude. Many women do not want to exchange one kind of oppression for another, but do want to be able to *talk* to someone who *listens* and to listen in return. But since this option needs care and trust, it doesn't have much appeal, and the difficulty remains a potential thorn in the side of many heterosexual friendships.

Women as friends with women

Women often express their surprise the first time they experience a group just how supportive women can be to each other. It is true that we have an enormous capacity for caring and for finding ways to pleasure. We can be very creative and imaginative in inventing little ways to show affection. We often go to infinite pains to find what will please, taking a lot of pleasure ourselves in doing so. We can listen, we understand that people have feelings, we are able to give a lot of attention to our friends which sometimes appears effortless to the receiver. We can be naturally excellent friends. Unfortunately, friendship between women at all levels often founders.

The first recognizable obstacle is a matter of *priorities*. Women who enjoy a close relationship find that once one or both enters into any committed sexual relationship, the friendship dwindles into comparative insignificance. Lack of time is the excuse. The difficulty can stem from a fear of asserting one's wish and need to spend time with a friend. This after all is for ourselves and therefore, like many other aspects of our lives, is superseded by responsibilities to others. Nor is it surprising that women friends are dispensable when we have been conditioned for so long to value the opinions and approval of men and when attachment to a man offers *real* status. Sex, falling in love, the 'real thing' are what matters, so the powder-room theme can still dominate the quality of time spent with other women. We chat inconsequentially while knowing we will eventually be recalled into the inner sanctum. As long as there is a possibility of being recalled, many women will refuse to take women's friendship seriously but view it as a pastime or a comfort in hard times rather than a commitment which needs to be nurtured. This is bolstered by a tendency when we do spend time together to talk exclusively about the others in our lives – children, husbands, partners, people in general – whether in defiance or deference, to focus exclusively on others. In this way many opportunities to establish direct communication are lost because we avoid talking about ourselves.

Deepening a friendship encounters a further obstacle of *competition*. At home or at work, friendship is acceptable, even enjoyable, until there is a suspicion that the woman will be attractive to your husband or be promoted over your head. I am sure many of us have at times short-sightedly flirted or had affairs with married men without realizing how this reinforces the expectation that when it comes to the prize, we fight dirty with little thought of loyalty or concern that as women we help make each other dispensable.

Strangely enough, one of our greatest gifts as women can also hinder intimacy. We learn to anticipate others' needs, to reach out in care and empathy, to love, to soothe, to heal. Because of this resource, many women experience very strong, positive support from each other, particularly in times of crisis or illness. This is powerful and female but can become compulsive. Sometimes, as women, we reach out to another in distress, not out of a genuine recognition of the other's need but out of guilt. When we are motivated by guilt, it is useful to remember that guilt is often a sign of unexpressed anger: anger held back and turned inwards with the result that we find it difficult to ask or receive something for ourselves. It has almost become second nature to deny our own needs.

We have become so strongly identified with the caring side of ourselves that we forget that an equally important aspect of loving is confronting. A lot of this stems from a general lack of assertive skills; we feel unable to be direct, to say no, to express feeling hurt or irritated by someone's behaviour, or to set limits because we are anxious to appear ever-caring and supportive and do not want to be hurtful. Handling, or rather not handling, our own and each other's anger undermines many of our relationships with other women. This affects individual friendships and relationships in a wider context. Women's groups of all kinds, consciousness raising, self-help, special interests, professional campaigning groups can be weakened by anger which is never openly addressed as an issue.

From past experience many of us remember and carry over a lot of anger towards women. From our mothers onwards, we have inherited a backlog of anger which is fuelled by the present. Many of us feel a frustration of personal power and of personal momentum. Lack of choice and recognition makes us angry. Contact with women stirs up old resentments as well as challenging new and fragile identities. It is easy to see why we are so susceptible. Fellow victims often despise each other to start with. And in trying to climb out, we can want to tread over each other, hold each other back or feel infuriated by those who just won't move! We feel let down by other women. We have learned not to trust and to tread warily around each other: we don't want to provoke another woman's anger because we fear it. Many women feel that another woman's anger is much more vicious, much more deadly than a man's anger. This confirms the suspicion that all women are potential bitches. Which is true, of course, except that it doesn't denote an intrinsic nastiness: it is simply the result of an inability to express anger assertively.

We feel more at home with an aggressive expression of anger which blames and seeks revenge; or with a passive expression – keep quiet and agree, there is no point, everything is useless, so instead of making a fuss, complain all the more loudly about the unfairness of being a victim. There is even prestige attached to oppression. Some women vie with each other to claim who has been the most oppressed in her life: an inverted status which awards the winner who has suffered most the reward of most sympathy and respect.

We do not encourage assertive expression of anger. If a woman gets angry, we turn away and negate it, perhaps thinking how silly or uncontrolled she looks. Or we analyze it or smooth it over. Tears are acceptable, not roars. We do this to our daughters, friends, sisters, mothers, patients, clients – women everywhere. We do not feel comfortable with emerging rage. A woman who takes power for herself and rejects the role of victim, acknowledging her responsibility, is unusual enough to be quite unsettling at times.

Imperfection. A further drawback to women's friendship is that when we do go over the top or, even worse, get it *wrong*, we risk being judged destructive, venomous, dangerous or crazy. The support suddenly disappears. Women find it very difficult to make room to accept each other's mistakes (or their own), so the potential for disappointment, spoken or usually unspoken, is widespread. Surprisingly, we find it difficult to treat each other as equals. Too often, we follow one of only two options: treat women as dependent children or dependable mothers. With the former, we sustain helplessness or we encourage the 'child' to be rebellious: blame and attack! With the latter, we look to other women to be always loving, understanding, supportive and perfect. It isn't surprising that many women avoid direct contact with each other! But when we persist, the rewards are handsome and incontestable.

We can encourage each other to take charge of our lives. We can stop giving unwanted advice and taking over. We can allow each other to make mistakes without secretly condemning ourselves for falling short of some mythical ideal. We can learn to forgive each other. If we stop getting trapped by the stereotyped duality of women as either weak or strong, we see a powerful woman who is at the same time vulnerable. Most of all we must forgive ourselves our impatience and our mistakes in learning to be with each other. In the face of so much pressure to look only towards men, we often appear strangers in each other's eyes.

The anxiety of this experience can precipitate us too quickly into identifying with similarities in others. There are experiences which we share, but it is the *differences* that we fail to handle as well. We rush to the safety of shared suffering, shared feeling, shared ideas, shared oppression, shared anger. This has been a large part of the strength of the women's movement. But it leaves us ill-equipped to embrace and learn from differences. Our insecurity makes us hunger for labels and uniformity. Sharing an experience is enabling, but only goes so far. We are sometimes afraid to learn from awkwardness, from disparity, from standing alone. So we keep ourselves inhibited in case we do something which is not acceptable, which shows us to be different in some way. The source of approval is inclusion and we fear losing that. Our fear becomes aggression towards others because in our need to belong, exclusion feels powerful.

But true power like true anger is not oppressive. It comes from oneself. It is not fuelled out of the misery of others or by excluding or denying others, or by seeking approval and acceptance of others. Only when we embrace aloneness can we look to each other directly, can we see, honour and care for another woman as she is. Our strength is not our own collectively until we make it our own individually.

18
Connections

It does all seem so difficult at times! If we had a firm sense of ourselves in the first place, things would be easier. But we don't. From very early on in our lives our identity and value lean on others. So for many of us, it takes some kind of upheaval – political, social or personal – to wake us up. Then we glimpse, as many women before us, that all is not well, that we, in fact, exist apart from all our roles, and that we have needs and feelings of our own. Our relationship with our body is an integral part of this awakening: until we own our bodies, we own nothing. This is a vital step but not the end of the story because we do not live in a vacuum. Consequently any sense of self is constantly under pressure from all the others in our lives.

For most of us, the balance between self and others remains a delicate one. It is particularly difficult in close relationships because when we open our hearts, we open ourselves to the risk of becoming dependent or of encouraging others to be dependent upon us. Most of us have a lot to learn about balancing love and independence.

It is difficult to believe that one can experience intimacy *and* independence: more often it feels as if one state automatically excludes the other. Being autonomous doesn't mean forgetting how to be close, to care, to love, to give. It simply means moving from a place of strength in oneself, respecting that there is a time for others and a time for self. Many women find autonomy difficult. Having made a move from total dependence on others, it still is a struggle. We teeter from one side to the other, longing for time on our own and then desperately missing closeness and security.

This time spent with oneself can be very strengthening. Many of us experience moments of this but that's all, just moments. Most of our time is devoted to others so we rarely detach ourselves long enough. Yet once we can detach ourselves and take the risk of extending these moments, we can feel the existence of an inner core, from which we can move out towards others and back again to the centre. Some call this inner core a spiritual self.

Sometimes we find it difficult to talk about this spiritual area of our lives without tripping into dogma. My own upbringing left me frustrated and alienated from religion because there was no room for discussion or consideration; it was simply a matter of *don't*. As a result I gave religion a wide and sceptical berth for many years, but in doing so have ignored for too long the spiritual side of myself and others. Since then I have met many women who are frustrated by a similar wish to feel some spiritual connection and commitment without being stifled by an oppressive doctrine. But we must talk of our spirit if we are to understand the wider loss of our bodies. It is in our bodies that our spirit abides and just as our bodies have been fragmented and damaged, so has our spirit. In reclaiming our bodies we take the first step towards spiritual healing.

In reclaiming our bodies, we reclaim our hearts. Loving is something we do extremely well. We simply need to include ourselves in that loving. Not a love that cares only for others and denies the self, not a love that smothers anger in oneself and others, not a love that is locked into a one-sided expression; this becomes a distortion of love.

If we reclaim our bodies and hearts, we reclaim our minds. I can hardly recall a woman who doesn't put down her intelligence, her ideas, her thoughts and opinions, so long have we learned to hide, to deny, to negate our capacity for creative or intellectual thought. If we reclaim our bodies, our hearts, our minds, we can then reclaim our spirit. Once we can do this individually, we can do so collectively. We can look beyond our immediate experience and see connections.

The first important connection is the recognition that the fear, mistrust and consequent mistreatment of women's bodies is not an isolated event. It is part of a continuous process which has its origins in very ordinary and accepted behaviour. Permission to treat women abusively begins with permission for the harmless comment; it extends with the unwanted touch on her head or arm; it is increased with the pat on her bottom or the squeeze of her breast; it finds completion in the hand around her throat and rape. From gawk to grope to grab are easy connecting steps. And yet we choose not to see.

This abuse isn't limited to a few psychotic individuals, nor can any one person be held to blame. For the most part, these attitudes are quite unconscious. It is easy enough to point to obvious advertisements or jokes or calendars or publications which are offensive but consider some of the more unlikely connections.

A social worker is reluctant to commit a father he knows is sexually abusing his daughter because he isn't quite sure that it isn't her fault; a policeman is slow to take action when a wife is being battered by her husband because he feels the man is being provoked; a lawyer persists in getting a child witness to recall every detail of an abusive attack when the evidence of the offender's guilt is quite clear, because he suspects that she has a vivid imagination; a judge grants the rapist a lenient sentence because he is sure that the woman got what she deserved looking the way she did; a priest reproaches a woman for considering contraception because he doesn't see a person already over-stressed and exhausted but sees only a woman's body which he believes has one sole function in life; a consultant allows women patients in his care to be examined vaginally by medical students while she is anaesthetized for a completely different operation because he cannot see it does any harm.

Attitudes like these don't just constitute a little wrinkle in society which can easily be ironed out. The very depth and breadth of the fear and mistrust of women's bodies, and its consequences, are more than we can take in. It is frightening to acknowledge these connections so we opt for closing our eyes and hoping it will all go away! It is not easy either to believe our perceptions when everything is denied and dismissed and logically explained away. But rational thinking doesn't help explain what we see through our senses. It doesn't help explain our intuitive wisdom.

And this very wisdom has been devalued both individually and collectively, as whole cultures based on intuitive belief systems have been crushed by aggression. The associated values, wisdom and skills of these cultures have all been trampled underfoot by the cash-hungry stampede. And so if we look at our world, we see that many human attributes and qualities traditionally considered female have been downgraded in favour of more 'masculine' attributes. What is more, we have lost sight of their original meaning and value. The quality of compassion, for example – loving through barriers and divisions, simply loving the person within, has degenerated into pity and patronage. The quality of receptivity has slid dangerously in the direction of flabbiness; a total inability to confront, a loss of pride and defiance, failure to set any limits whatsoever. The compulsion to accommodate has left many women unable to be single-minded about anything at all. Flexibility of attitudes and approach has degenerated into blandness. Politically, women are bland. A few carry the burden of effort for the many. The few get tired and disillusioned because when it comes to the crunch, the many won't risk putting themselves on the line and making a commitment to any form of action.

Another connection is that between women and nature. This is nothing new and it's easy to see the parallel. The earth has always been viewed as alternately nurturing and uncontrollable: a woman's body has been viewed as either motherly or dangerous. For many centuries a lot of effort has been put into taming the excesses of both! Consequently mistreatment of women is mirrored in the mistreatment of the natural environment. Untold billions of tons of pollutants have been discharged into the atmosphere; fish are now dying from liver and skin cancer from pollutants in the waters of the world; forests are felled, destroying the balance of natural environment; productive land is ploughed up, soil is over-used; the earth's resources are overmined leaving it barren and exhausted. Each act has been carried out without awareness or care for the consequences. It is when we stop looking only ahead towards future progress and look *around* instead, and above and underneath at all the unseen systems which have been irreversibly affected, that we begin to understand the meaning of the word 'connections'.

As women, we have become alienated from our bodies and, as a race, we have become alienated from the natural environment. As we have become less concerned with the integrity of life and death, we now see in our world a profound disrespect for both. Death has become another challenge to master and control, so human dignity disappears from both dying and living. A care for women is connected with a concern for the earth. The affinity is a natural one so it is not surprising that there is an affinity between feminism and ecology. As the Greenham women have shown, women are concerned and prepared to fight in their own way for the value of life and peace. In 1982, a spokesman for the Centre for Science and Environment in India, when reporting on attempts to maintain the Himalayan forests, said that every single achievement had been due to the women who had stopped the men from cutting the trees. 'When environmental degradation takes place,' he said, 'it is the women who walk further.'

Resilience is a remarkable quality and it sometimes astounds me how women do survive and flourish. We have tremendous power and energy when our spirit is fired. Yet most of the time, we are exhausted with the simple demands of living and caring for others so that there is little or no time for us to make our voices heard or our impact felt.

My passion arises from a deep sorrow at the loss of our beauty and from an equally deep anger that the power, force, flexibility, richness, diversity and above all, the dignity of women, have been lost. The virtue of suffering, the ability to allow, to take in, has become distorted into women being unable to say 'no more'. The real meaning of suffering is a noble quality, not one which demeans, belittles, trivializes, overburdens.

The extraordinary aspect of all this is that as women we *know*. I have always recognized that in all my work I have been teaching women something they knew already at some deeper level. Their response seems to spring from an ancient and secret wisdom which is kept hidden for most of the time. This is in fact the key – to discover our strength, our bodies, our real beauty and our power is not to start from scratch but to reclaim, to rediscover, to affirm what is *already* there.

We do not need to take to the barricades. We just need to acknowledge that what we see within offers a true reflection of what is without. Until we do, we remain an endangered species, our bodies exploited, our skills unused, our wisdom unrecognized.

The recent eruptions of two volcanoes (Mount St Helen in 1980 in Washington State, USA and El Chicon, Mexico, in 1982) finally made the scientific establishment take note: the after-effects forced them to consider the consequences of a nuclear winter. The warning of those volcanoes offers an encouraging symbolism. We too can burst forth, in anger at what we don't like, in affirmation of and love for what we hold dear. Instead of being pillars of society we could use our own strength and stand up ourselves. Looking from within we can see that we belong to something which doesn't demand conformity, sweetness or pretence: it asks only that we grasp the truth within ourselves.

Further Information
Further Reading
Index

Further Information

1. If you want further information about **sexuality** or **assertiveness training classes** near your home, please write to the author care of the publishers, enclosing a stamped addressed envelope.

2. In Chapter 10, a reference is made to a process by which we can learn to release feelings physically in a safe context. This refers to a set of skills called **co-counselling**. For further information about co-counselling, please write to the author as above.

3. **Vibrators.** Two vibrators currently on the market are the Pifco Massager and Workout by House of Carmen. The Pifco model is sold at most chemists; the House of Carmen model is sold at branches of Alders and Underwoods for those who live near London. Otherwise contact House of Carmen directly: House of Carmen, Mexborough, South Yorkshire S64 8AJ, tel: (0709) 582402.

4. You can buy a plastic **speculum** from John Bell and Croyden (Surgical Division), 54 Wigmore Street, London W1H 0AU, tel: (01) 935 3555.

Further Reading

Barbach, Lonnie Garfield, *For Yourself – The Fulfilment of Female Sexuality*, Doubleday, 1975. Clear and comprehensive.

Brown, RitaMae, *Ruby Fruit Jungle*. A readable first-hand account of growing up as a lesbian in a heterosexual culture.

Chesler, Phyllis, *With Child*, Crowell, 1979. A personal diary describing the experiences of the pregnancy and birth of her first child.

Cousins, Jane, *Make it Happy*, Penguin, 1980. A very readable book about sex, written for teenagers

Dodson, Betty, *Liberating Masturbation*, 1975. A small illustrated booklet encouraging a positive approach to se. pleasuring.

Dworkin, Andrea, *Pornography – Men Possessing Women*, Women's Press, 1981. A forceful and provocative account of the damaging effect of pornography

Federation of Feminist Women's Health Centers, *A New View of A Woman's Body*, Simon and Schuster, 1981. A clear and comprehensive guide to women's physiology

French, Marilyn, *The Women's Room*, Sphere, 1979. An addictive novel.

Friday, Nancy, *My Secret Garden*, Virago/Quartet, 1975. An account of women's sexual fantasies.

Griffin, Susan, *Woman and Nature – The Roaring inside Her*, Women's Press, 1984. Evocative, original account of the link between the pollution of the earth and the negative attitudes to women's bodies.

Heiman and Lo Piccolo, *Becoming Orgasmic*, Prentice-Hall, 1976. A step-by-step plan for discovering masturbation and orgasm.

Hooper, Anne, *The Body Electric*, Virago, 1980. The first English book about the experience of learning to reach orgasm and attending a pre-orgasmic group.

Kerr, Carmen, *Sex for Women*, Grove Press, 1977. A transactional analysis approach containing useful concepts about women's sexual 'games'.

Kolbenschlag, Madonna, *Kiss Sleeping Beauty Goodbye*, Bantam, 1981. A compelling and lucid account of the effect of cultural myths on women's behaviour.

Martin, Del and Lyon, Phyllis, *Lesbian Women*, Bantam, 1972, A classic.

Meulenbelt, Anja, *For Ourselves*, Sheba, 1981. Recommended for a feminist perspective on women and sexuality.

Orbach, Susie, *Fat is a Feminist Issue*, Hamlyn 1979. An excellent book on the relationship between body image, weight and sexuality.

Phillips, Angela and Rakusen, Jill, *Our Bodies, Ourselves*, Penguin, 1978. An English edition of the American original. A good reference book to own.

Rich, Adrienne, *Of Woman Born: Motherhood as Experience and Institution*, Virago, 1977. Probably the most important book to have come out of the women's movement. A must.

Sanders, Deidre, *The Woman Book of Love and Sex*, Sphere, 1985. A report of 15,000 married and unmarried women's answers to a questionnaire in *Woman* magazine

Shuttle, Penelope and Redgrove, Peter, *The Wise Wound*, Gollancz, 1978. A beautifully written book about menstruation.

Walker, Alice, *The Color Purple*, Women's Press, 1983. A wonderful and moving novel.

Zilbergeld, Bernie, *Men and Sex*, Souvenir, 1979. A clear and comprehensive guide for men about male sexuality.

Index